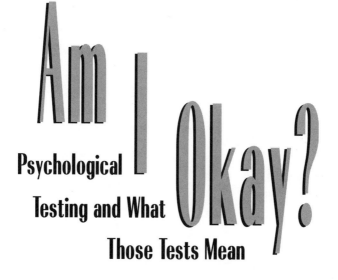

Am I Okay?

Psychological Testing and What Those Tests Mean

Am I Okay?
Psychological Testing and What Those Tests Mean

Anorexia Nervosa:
Starving for Attention

Child Abuse and Neglect:
Examining the Psychological Components

Conduct Unbecoming:
Hyperactivity, Attention Deficit, and Disruptive Behavior Disorders

Cutting the Pain Away:
Understanding Self-Mutilation

Disorders First Diagnosed in Childhood

Drowning Our Sorrows:
Psychological Effects of Alcohol Abuse

Life Out of Focus:
Alzheimer's Disease and Related Disorders

The Mental Effects of Heroin

Mental Illness and Its Effects on School and Work Environments

Out of Control:
Gambling and Other Impulse-Control Disorders

Personality Disorders

Psychological Disorders Related to Designer Drugs

■ **Psychological Effects of Cocaine and Crack Addiction**

■ **Schizophrenia:**
Losing Touch with Reality

■ **Sexual Disorders**

■ **Sibling Rivalry:**
Relational Problems Involving Brothers and Sisters

■ **Sleep Disorders**

■ **Smoke Screen:**
Psychological Disorders Related to Nicotine Use

■ **Strange Visions:**
Hallucinogen-Related Disorders

■ **Through a Glass Darkly:**
The Psychological Effects of Marijuana and Hashish

■ **The Tortured Mind:**
The Many Faces of Manic Depression

■ **Uneasy Lives:**
Understanding Anxiety Disorders

■ **When Families Fail:**
Psychological Disorders and Dysfunctional Families

■ **A World Upside Down and Backwards:**
Reading and Learning Disorders

THE ENCYCLOPEDIA OF PSYCHOLOGICAL DISORDERS

Senior Consulting Editor Carol C. Nadelson, M.D.
Consulting Editor Claire E. Reinburg

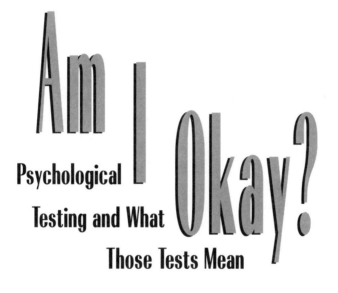

Am I Okay?

Psychological Testing and What Those Tests Mean

Dwayne E. Pickels

CHELSEA HOUSE PUBLISHERS
Philadelphia

The ENCYCLOPEDIA OF PSYCHOLOGICAL DISORDERS provides up-to-date information on the history of, causes and effects of, and treatment and therapies for problems affecting the human mind. The titles in this series are not intended to take the place of the professional advice of a psychiatrist or mental health care professional.

Chelsea House Publishers
Editor in Chief: Stephen Reginald
Production Manager: Pamela Loos
Art Director: Sara Davis
Director of Photography: Judy L. Hasday
Managing Editor: James D. Gallagher
Senior Production Editor: J. Christopher Higgins

Staff for AM I OKAY? PSYCHOLOGICAL TESTING AND WHAT THOSE TESTS MEAN
Prepared by P. M. Gordon Associates, Philadelphia
Picture Researcher: P. M. Gordon Associates
Associate Art Director: Takeshi Takahashi
Cover Designer: Emiliano Begnardi

The Chelsea House World Wide Web address is
http://www.chelseahouse.com

First Printing

9 8 7 6 5 4 3 2 1

Library of Congress Cataloging-in-Publication Data

Pickels, Dwayne E.

Am I Okay?: Psychological testing and what those tests mean / by Dwayne E. Pickels.
    p.   cm. — (Encyclopedia of psychological disorders)
Includes bibliographical references and index.
Summary: An examination of the history and types of psychological testing, and a discussion of what the results mean.
ISBN 0-7910-5319-9
1. Psychological tests—Juvenile Literature. 2. Psychological tests—History—Juvenile literature [1. Psychological tests.] I. Title. II. Series.
BF176.P53   1999
150'.28'7—dc21   99-30473
                                                                        CIP

CONTENTS

Introduction by Carol C. Nadelson, M.D.   6

The Role of Psychological Testing: An Overview   9

1   What's in a Name?   13

2   A Brief History of Psychological Testing   19

3   Testing for Intelligence   29

4   Testing for Personality   45

5   Testing Children   59

6   Testing for Interests and Employment   71

7   The Meaning and Future of Psychological Testing   79

Appendix: For More Information   84

Appendix: Selected Psychological Tests   86

Bibliography   89

Further Reading   91

Glossary   92

Index   94

PSYCHOLOGICAL DISORDERS AND THEIR EFFECT

CAROL C. NADELSON, M.D.
PRESIDENT AND CHIEF EXECUTIVE OFFICER,
The American Psychiatric Press

There are a wide range of problems that are considered psychological disorders, including mental and emotional disorders, problems related to alcohol and drug abuse, and some diseases that cause both emotional and physical symptoms. Psychological disorders often begin in early childhood, but during adolescence we see a sharp increase in the number of people affected by these disorders. It has been estimated that about 20 percent of the U.S. population will have some form of mental disorder sometime during their lifetime. Some psychological disorders appear following severe stress or trauma. Others appear to occur more often in some families and may have a genetic or inherited component. Still other disorders do not seem to be connected to any cause we can yet identify. There has been a great deal of attention paid to learning about the causes and treatments of these disorders, and exciting new research has taught us a great deal in the past few decades.

The fact that many new and successful treatments are available makes it especially important that we reject old prejudices and outmoded ideas that consider mental disorders to be untreatable. If psychological problems are identified early, it is possible to prevent serious conse-quences. We should not keep these problems hidden or feel shame that we or a member of our family has a mental disorder. Some people believe that something they said or did caused a mental disorder. Some people think that these disorders are "only in your head" so that you could "snap out of it" if you made the effort. This type of thinking implies that a treatment is a matter of willpower or motivation. It is a terrible burden for someone who is suffering to be blamed for his or her misery, and often people with psychological disorders are not treated compassionately. We hope that the information in this book will teach you about various mental illnesses.

The problems covered in the volumes in the ENCYCLOPEDIA OF PSYCHOLOGICAL DISORDERS were selected because they are of particular importance to young adults, because they affect them directly or because they affect family and friends. There are individual volumes on reading disorders, attention deficit and disruptive behavior disorders, and dementia—all of these are related to our abilities to learn and integrate information from the world around us. There are books on drug abuse that provide useful information about the effects of these drugs and treatments that are available for those individuals who have drug problems. Some of the books concentrate on one of the most common mental disorders, depression. Others deal with eating disorders, which are dangerous illnesses that affect a large number of young adults, especially women.

Most of the public attention paid to these disorders arises from a particular incident involving a celebrity that awakens us to our own vulnerability to psychological problems. These incidents of celebrities or public figures revealing their own psychological problems can also enable us to think about what we can do to prevent and treat these types of problems.

Psychological testing can provide information that psychologists and parents need in order to make the best decisions for a child's future. This test is being administered one-on-one—one tester to one subject.

THE ROLE OF PSYCHOLOGICAL TESTING: AN OVERVIEW

One hundred years ago, few people had heard of psychological tests. Today, such tests are commonly found in schools, work-places, counseling centers, and hospitals, where they are used to measure intelligence, aptitude, personality, and occupational interests. The range of psychological tests includes those that attempt to determine a person's suitability for a job or promotion, measure overall mental health, show whether brain damage is present, demonstrate what a person has accomplished, or predict an individual's future behavior.

When professionals administer psychological tests responsibly, the tests provide information that helps create an environment in which people can develop their abilities to the greatest extent possible. Parents and teachers can determine how a child best learns. Employers can create a productive working environment. Individuals can follow career paths that lead to personally fulfilling occupations. And family members can better understand and appreciate one another.

But from the time that psychological testing first began, critics have expressed doubts about its effectiveness. Some have questioned the reliability of psychological tests. Others have wondered whether the results actually reflect what the tests claim to measure. Still others have pointed to *biases* (preferences or inclinations, especially those that prevent impartial judgment) in the tests. They argue that many of the tests—which they view as targeted toward white, middle-class Americans—are a better measure of how much a test subject understands about suburban life than of anything else.

Some people have also raised the question of how much schools and employers should rely on test results when evaluating prospective students and workers. They have pointed to the fact that the anxiety and stress of taking a test sometimes causes people to panic.

Sometimes psychological tests are combined with other tools in an effort to identify a problem. This therapist's interview with family members is part of a psychological assessment.

Consequently, test results may not accurately reflect the subjects' capabilities.

For decades, experts have constantly refined psychological tests and the methods used to create them, seeking to eliminate flaws in test designs. In addition, researchers periodically update the tests in order to reflect changes in language and technology.

In spite of these efforts, concerns about psychological tests remain. As tests increasingly become computerized, new questions of privacy and confidentiality arise. Parents wonder whether appropriate steps are being taken to protect their children's test scores from falling into the hands of other students. Employees want assurances that computerized personnel files can't be accessed by unauthorized persons.

As the field of psychological testing enters a new millennium, it faces many challenges. Continued modification will be needed so that these tests can better measure human behavior and give people the tools they need to improve their lives.

Many people link the words psychological testing *to negative images and experiences, such as stressful school testing situations. However, psychological tests are simply tools that measure and define various aspects of human behavior in order to help people get the most out of life.*

1

WHAT'S IN
A NAME?

The words *psychological testing* produce widely varying images in different people's minds. Some people conjure up images from old horror movies in which torturous mental prodding and probing uncover proof of insanity or the presence of some mental disorder. The images may include a "mad" scientist who mutters, "Very interesting," as he locks a hapless victim into a sadistic-looking sensory-deprivation cell in which the subject will undergo long and agonizing experiments.

Other people get their ideas about psychological testing from what they hear in the news. Following a terrible crime, reporters often announce that suspects are undergoing psychological evaluation. After hearing repeatedly about such tests, some people begin to associate psychological testing with the determination of whether an individual is criminally insane. Only crazy people need to take psychological tests, they think.

The word *test* itself frequently brings to mind school experiences in which a test could decide whether a person would pass or fail a particular class or even an entire grade. The term *test* also reminds some people of medical settings, where doctors examine patients with instruments or take blood samples to evaluate how well the body systems are working.

With the association of such negative images, it's not hard to understand why many people shy away from the suggestion of psychological testing. But these attempts to measure human behavior, abilities, and problems and to make predictions about future performance are not as forbidding as they may sound. Most psychological tests aren't used to ferret out abnormalities. Instead, they are designed and used to provide a better understanding of precisely what "normal" is—a question that professionals still debate.

Simply put, psychology is the study of human behavior. Psychologists try to achieve many goals in the pursuit of that study. They define and describe human behavior, tracing its causes and predicting its future. They examine not only people's actions but also the results of those actions. Some psychologists even attempt to modify and control human behavior. And one of the basic ways in which psychologists carry out their research is through testing. Psychological testing provides a way to measure and define various aspects of human behavior.

Given the complex nature of human beings and the wide variety of behaviors they exhibit, studying behavior is no easy task. In fact, the theories and experiments that produce a particular result in a test subject on one day can produce an entirely different result in that same subject on another day. Results also vary from one subject to another. However, psychologists have developed various methods of detecting and measuring characteristics of their subjects. These techniques can help account for such variables as the kind of day a person may be having, giving experts the means to produce more consistent, and accurate, results.

Psychological testing has become so common in our society that most people have undergone such testing at one point or another in their lives. Schools use the tests to measure intelligence and academic achievement and to predict future performance. Employers turn to the tests to evaluate an individual's work style or aptitude for a job. Therapists administer personality tests to assist them in providing patients with marriage and family counseling.

A "GOOD" TEST

Any aspect of human behavior that a test measures must be strictly defined and examined in its proper context. In other words, tests need to be both reliable and valid.

Reliability refers to how well a test produces the same results under the same set of circumstances for the same person. Barring conditions such as unperceived changes in the subject, tests that produce different results for the same subject are often considered unreliable. Reliable tests produce reasonably consistent results.

Validity, on the other hand, simply indicates how well a test measures what it is designed to measure. A valid test, for example, would not seek to measure a person's intelligence by examining his or her annual income. Instead, it would examine skills such as reasoning ability. A valid test to evaluate a student's mathematical skills might include mathematical equations.

In our crowded world, it has become necessary to develop tests that can be administered to numerous people at once. A single individual with little training can administer a standardized test to a large group.

Another element of a good test is *administration*. This simply indicates the way the test is presented to its subjects. In most cases, an individual tester gives, or administers, a test to either an individual or a group.

When a test becomes standardized, one person with relatively little training is able to administer the test and organize the results. In *standardized tests* experts carefully define the procedures for administration and scoring and select the content through a rigorous process. The Stanford Achievement Test, the Metropolitan Achievement Test (MAT), the California Achievement Test (CAT), the Comprehensive Test of Basic Skills, and the Iowa Test of Basic Skills are examples of standardized tests that are widely administered to elementary school students in

A good test must have established norms—standards that indicate what the normal or expected performance on the test should be. Here a researcher uses a pie chart to determine norms as a test is being developed.

the United States. The Scholastic Assessment Tests (SAT), which are also standardized, allow high school graduates who are applying to various colleges and universities to take a single entrance exam.

Standardized tests are useful in cases where large numbers of people are being tested simultaneously. In these situations a single tester cannot interact with all the subjects at once, and standardized tests eliminate the need for such individual involvement. Because factors such as motivation and distraction can cause a subject in a large test group to perform below his or her abilities, however, standardized tests have been developed in ways that minimize the impact of such problems.

Other tests have been designed to be administered one-on-one—one tester to one subject. The people who administer these tests are highly trained. They are capable of interacting with an individual subject in ways that will bring his or her performance to the highest possible level.

The final characteristic of a good test is the establishment of *norms*. Norms make it possible to compare one individual's performance on a test with the performance of a larger group. For instance, an individual eighth grader's results on a test can be compared with the results of all eighth graders who have taken the same test. Researchers usually determine norms while a test is being developed. They analyze and debate the initial results and then make changes to the test. This process continues until the developers are comfortable that the norms represent what the standard, normal, or expected performance on the test should be. Once this mark has been established, experts can compare a new score against it to determine whether an individual's performance is average, above average, or below average.

The results of the standardized SAT, which is taken by students before they apply to a college or university for admission, provide a common example of the use of norms. The results of this test provide students with scores for each of two test sections (verbal and math) and compare these scores to those of other test takers. A percentile rank tells what percentage of people taking the test received a lower score than did the individual test taker. A person who scores in the 80th percentile knows that 80 percent of the people who took the same test received a lower score. A person who scores in the 50th percentile knows that half the people taking the test received a lower score.

Some tests are simple, others are complex, but all are designed for specific types of measurement. Based on the information that these tests provide, the conclusions reached depend on the discretion, responsibility, and skill of those who administer the tests. When psychological tests are used correctly, they are an important tool that can help people get the most from what life has to offer them.

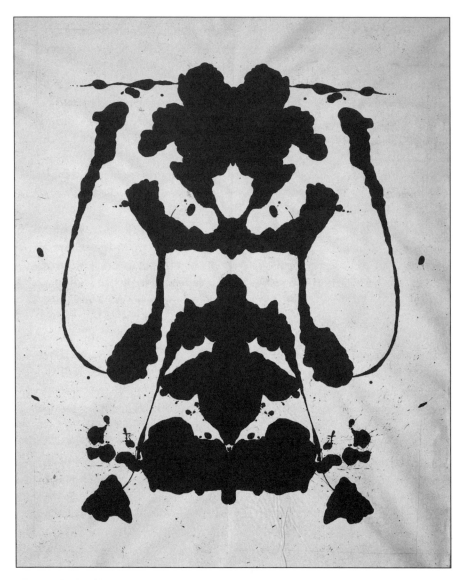

The Rorschach Inkblot Test, which uses printed shapes to measure personality, has become part of the popular culture. Shown here is a painting by Andy Warhol entitled "Rorschach, 1984."

2

A BRIEF HISTORY OF PSYCHOLOGICAL TESTING

S ome sources claim that the roots of psychological testing run deeper than modern civilization itself. In fact, some experts trace testing back as far as 2200 B.C. Ancient Chinese dynasties are said to have used formal tests to help determine assignments to various governmental posts. The same sort of evaluation has probably taken place on an informal basis in any society where decisions about who receives a job are based on factors other than brute force or political power. Throughout history, leaders have asked themselves and their advisers, "Who is best for the job?"

There have always been a number of reasons for wanting to know something about "what makes people tick." Who could we rely on, or who would be best suited for combat? Who could represent us to the gods? Who among us should oversee the harvest? Who would be fit to rule or serve as an ambassador to other kingdoms? These questions were usually not answered simply on the basis of who was best qualified. But whenever it was possible to use such a democratic approach, it became apparent that there should be logical ways of learning what traits and abilities one or more people might possess and how they might use them in a given situation.

THE OLD-FASHIONED WAY

Some psychologists still assert that the best way to determine and measure an individual's abilities, traits, and interests is the old-fashioned way, through *natural observation*. In other words, we simply watch people in their natural environments to learn what they are like. Take friends or family members, for example. For the most part, if we have paid any attention at all over the time we've been with our families and friends, we know their likes and dislikes. We have a sense of what makes them happy or sad, and we probably know how

Natural observation—which has been in use since before the development of psycholog-ical tests—can be an effective, though time-consuming, way of learning about a subject. Here researchers observe children at play.

they would react in some situations. This is knowledge that we have attained through extended periods of personal observation.

Although this approach has its merits, psychologists usually don't examine close friends or family members. Their subjects are more likely to be strangers about whom the scientists know very little, if anything, prior to working with them. Thus, a psychologist needs some means of obtaining information about the aptitudes, abilities, or traits of these individuals. The natural observation method simply takes too long in most situations.

When psychologists in the late 1800s and early 1900s determined that they needed a faster way to learn about a subject, they found it necessary to refine some of the ways that they gathered information. Thus, the psychological test was born. Over time, psychological testing became a specialty in itself. Some psychologists focused on developing the science of giving and creating tests that other psychologists could apply to real-life situations.

CRITICISMS OF TESTING

As psychological testing developed, so did its critics. To this day, people find fault with various aspects of testing. Some critics object to the purposes of psychological testing and the use of its results as voraciously as others challenge its methods. Although specific tests face specific criticisms, some basic problems in testing can be separated into the following general categories.

1. Questions about testing methods

Some critics have questioned tests' reliance on the responses of subjects, who may give answers that reflect what they think the tester wants to hear rather than what they really feel. This concern causes uncertainty about whether test results reflect the way a subject *wants* to be perceived rather than his or her true thoughts or feelings.

In other cases, subjects may face circumstances such as language barriers that unfairly impact their performance. Some critics express concern about academic achievement tests, which use standard English, that are administered to groups that include immigrants from non-English-speaking countries or children who live in urban or rural areas where standard English is not commonly spoken. In these cases, a poor performance on such tests may result from a language barrier rather than from some lack of the intelligence or problem-solving skills that the tests are designed to measure.

Still other subjects may have an underlying fear of taking tests. This anxiety may hamper their performance, affecting their ability to concentrate or increasing the time they take to answer each question—perhaps even preventing them from completing the test in the time allotted. Under such circumstances, test results are unlikely to reflect true abilities.

The widespread computerization of tests has raised new questions of confidentiality. The concern that unauthorized persons might gain access to personal information has become a serious issue.

2. Questions about the purpose of testing

The purpose of each test, as well as the way the test administrator intends to use the results, must be clearly and honestly defined. Why is the test being administered? What is it designed to determine? Who will have access to the results? These questions are important to both the individual test subjects and society as a whole.

In cases such as the testing of schoolchildren, protecting the subjects and ensuring that test results remain confidential are of the utmost concern. As technology provides new ways to access information every day, the danger that information will be used inappropriately increases. Privacy issues, including who might have access to personal data and what they might do with that information, are serious concerns in today's society. In the school environment, for example, parents and children need to know that clerical workers and other school employees who use office computers will not be able to obtain personal data. Only with the assurance that authorized personnel alone will have access to confidential information can parents and children feel secure that this information will remain confidential.

POPULAR PSYCHOLOGY

Despite—or perhaps because of—the stigmas and fears attributed to the concept of psychological testing, this field of study has caught the eye of popular culture. Testing has been the subject of many fictional works, such as novels and films, and has also become fodder for television shows and comedy routines.

Some of the better-known psychological tests have found their way into the popular culture as well. They have become ingrained in the common knowledge base, though they are not always identified by name. Mention the name Hermann Rorschach among an average group of people, and one or two may be very familiar with his contribution to the study of human behavior in the early 1900s. They may know Rorschach as the developer of the Rorschach Inkblot Test, which uses printed shapes to measure personality. Others in the group may be vaguely familiar with the name, realizing that it has something to do with inkblots. Still others may be familiar with the inkblots without recognizing the name. The remaining few may have no clue about who Rorschach was or what purposes his inkblots serve.

Another example is the term *IQ*. Most people's knowledge of the term

IT'S ALL IN THE QUESTION

One of the aspects of testing that requires the most refinement is how a particular question is stated. Researchers have learned that the exact wording of a question can greatly change how the same person will respond to it.

"Do you like going to school?" and "Do you like getting an education?" may sound very similar. But a student who gets teased at school or does not like his or her teacher may answer "no" to the first question and "yes" to the second.

Similarly, although many people may answer "yes" to "Do you like baseball?" as well as to "Do you like to play baseball?" the questions differ slightly. Some baseball fans love watching the game but hate playing it themselves.

consists of only the fact that it is used to describe a person's intelligence. Those who have studied human behavior in even a limited capacity are probably aware that IQ stands for "intelligence quotient." Fewer are likely to recall, however, that the quotient was the result of a mathematical equation developed in the early 1900s by two French psychologists— Alfred Binet and Theodore Simon (discussed in more detail in chapter 3).

Binet and Simon developed the measuring technique that we now call the IQ test. Their formula was simply that IQ was equal to the sum of the subject's mental age divided by his or her chronological age and then multiplied by 100. The original method has undergone some revision over the years, particularly at Stanford University, where the term "intelligence quotient" was actually coined about a decade after the publication of Binet and Simon's formula. Yet the term IQ remains in popular use and IQ tests remain one of the best known of the many psychological tests to which the general populace is exposed.

TYPES OF TESTS

Psychological tests have been developed not only to determine and measure aspects of human behavior, such as intelligence, ability, and personality, but also to develop an understanding of how humans acquire, interpret, and store information. Generally, psychological tests are divided into three primary categories: tests of ability or aptitude, measures of personality, and indicators of interests.

Tests of ability or aptitude seek to describe or measure intelligence, reasoning, or cognitive skills. Aptitude tests are designed to measure, or predict, what a subject may be capable of accomplishing or achieving with some degree of instruction or training, whereas achievement tests assess what skills or knowledge a subject already possesses. Often such tests are strictly timed and tailored to determine the maximum performance of a group or an individual.

Personality tests can be as deeply complex as those developed by university research teams or as superficial as a "date quiz" in a popular magazine. But whatever the format, they all seek to determine the various traits that make individuals unique. Personality tests are generally divided into objective and projective tests.

Objective tests ask a series of specific questions designed to be answered either by choosing "yes" or "no" or by selecting one of two or more possible responses. A single individual will often administer the test to a group of people.

One of the first objective tests, which was created early in the development of the science of psychological testing, was used to screen military recruits during World War I. That test contained 116 questions, including the following: Did you have a happy childhood? Have you ever been afraid of going insane? Does it make you uneasy to cross a bridge over a river? Developers designed this line of questioning to call attention to recruits who might exhibit behavior problems that would make them unacceptable for military service.

A more sophisticated and accurate test that is still widely used is the Minnesota Multiphasic Personality Inventory (MMPI). This test consists of more than 500 statements. The subject responds to each statement by indicating either "true," "false," or "cannot say."

Unlike objective tests, *projective tests* usually require one-on-one administration. The person taking the test is presented with a standardized set of stimuli (for example, the inkblots in the Rorschach Inkblot Test), and the subject's responses are analyzed. Because subjects must generally describe what they see, they have greater freedom in their responses than they have in objective tests. Many psychologists believe

Projective tests usually allow subjects greater leeway in their responses than objective tests. Here a tester asks a subject to describe a Rorschach inkblot.

that projective tests produce a more meaningful, accurate description of personality than objective tests; however, the results are more difficult to interpret.

Interest testing seeks to help people understand their interests and working styles. With this information, they are better equipped to pursue careers that will be personally satisfying. Institutions of higher learning use such tests to help students choose a field of concentration. Employers use the tests to screen job applicants and evaluate employees.

The designs, goals, and uses of an individual test often cross over into more than one of the three major psychological test categories. Even the difference between intelligence and aptitude, if one exists, may depend on whom you ask. Some tests that developers have designed to measure one aspect of human behavior may just as well measure another, depending on how the results are interpreted. In spite of these overlapping uses for tests, it is helpful to have a general understanding of the types of psychological tests and what those tests can accomplish.

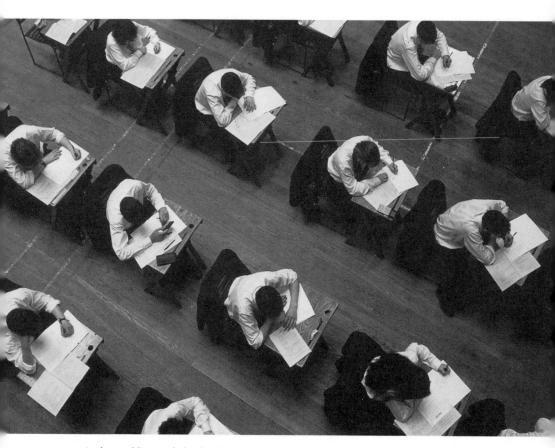

As the world's population has increased, so has the need for group IQ testing. Group tests are now commonly used to determine admission to branches of the U.S. military as well as to U.S. institutions of higher learning.

3

TESTING FOR INTELLIGENCE

Are you smart? If you are reading this book by your own choice, chances are you possess what some psychologists would consider average to above-average intelligence.

But perhaps a better, more scientific question would be "How smart are you?" Now we are no longer looking at the black-or-white, yes-or-no question "Are you smart?" or "Are you not smart?" Rather, we find ourselves examining a query most often portrayed in varying shades of gray, with no hard-and-fast answer. That is just where most aspects of human behavior (and its study) seem to fall.

Psychologists generally agree that *intelligence* has to do with an individual's ability to adapt to his or her environment. The abilities to solve problems, adjust to new situations, and learn new skills contribute to a person's intelligence. All of us possess a certain level of intelligence, but that intelligence may be expressed in different ways. Each individual has some unique set of abilities that may be better suited to one type of activity than to another.

In some cases, individuals whose mental ability is considered "normal" may not display their intelligence in ways that are immediately apparent to others. People may then label them falsely, asserting, for example, "She's stupid" or "He's not the sharpest knife in the drawer." The fact is, however, that relatively few people are, for lack of a better word, "stupid." For most people who are labeled as such, it's more than likely that their abilities and skills are simply not suited for the particular tasks by which they are presently being gauged. People who perform brilliantly in certain activities or pursuits may perform poorly in others. Conversely, people who strike us as dull or unintelligent in one situation may turn around and dazzle us with their genius in another.

Think about an automobile mechanic who can't distinguish the organ music that Johann Sebastian Bach composed in the first half of the 1700s from the piano concertos that Wolfgang Amadeus Mozart composed in the last half

People often demonstrate abilities that vary from one task to another. This mechanic, for example, may have great difficulty distinguishing the music of various classical composers but little difficulty repairing an automobile engine.

of that century. To concert pianists or symphony conductors who have studied classical music and the arts all of their lives, the mechanic may seem to be of below-average intelligence. But when it comes time to change the transmission in their car, they may develop a completely different view of the person.

This example is simplistic, of course, but it illustrates one of the biggest challenges in testing for intelligence. Individuals and entire societies are widely diverse and complex. They don't think alike, value or pursue the same ideals, or have the same resources from which to draw. People in different social surroundings have different forces influencing them—some of which encourage the expression of intelligence and some of which stifle it.

These variables create problems for the developers of intelligence tests. For a test to be reliable and valid, the "playing field" must be level. How can experts develop a test that doesn't include a bias toward people with particular lifestyles, economic backgrounds, or life experiences? The efforts of psychologists to overcome that obstacle constitute a large part of the story of the development of intelligence tests.

THE ROOTS OF INTELLIGENCE

In order to use the word *intelligence* properly, we need to consider it as more than a measure of how smart someone is. Intelligence involves how people gather or select knowledge and what kinds of choices they make in particular environments. Even then, we must remember that any one of a number of different options will often effectively handle whatever situation an individual faces. Two people who are equally intelligent may make different choices with equally effective results. Some options, however, produce quite negative results—a decision to commit an unlawful act, for example. Choices that cause harm are almost always wrong.

Most psychological tests do not set out to establish whether an individual is making right or wrong choices. They merely try to identify what choices a subject will make. This information may, in turn, help psychologists define or predict behavior in certain individuals. Consequently, there is some agreement about the benefit of measuring intellect, as complex as the concept is and as limited as our understanding of it may be.

Intelligence tests must not only produce reliable, consistent, valid information about a subject in a short amount of time; they must also convert that information into a format that can be compared with data collected from other subjects. Comparison is an important part of studying any kind of scientific data. Without a way to compare information that we derive from a test, the results are merely a collection of meaningless facts.

For example, if a man were to tell you that his best friend gave him $100, you might think that the friend was very generous, especially if the man told you that the friend was currently unemployed. But what if someone told you that the friend had recently won a lottery worth $37 million? You might form a very different opinion. What's worse, your conclusions might not be accurate in either case. You don't have enough data. You need to know more.

One very good way to learn more is to compare what you are studying with what you already know. In the field of psychological testing, experts often accomplish this by establishing norms (as explained in chapter 1). When developers create a test, they administer it to a test group, which yields results that are more or less anticipated. The developers then use these results to establish parameters, guidelines, and other tools to create a set of norms. In other words, the test group produces results that certain types of people who will later take the test are likely to produce. This process continues until the developers are satisfied that their test will reliably accomplish what they want it to accomplish. Over time, tests have become more sophisticated and more sensitive. Let's look at how this process has worked in intelligence tests.

THE GROWTH OF INTELLIGENCE THEORIES

Over the centuries, scientists, philosophers, and physicians have proposed theories concerning the nature of intelligence. Galen (c. 130–200), a Greek-born and -educated physician who practiced in Rome, put forth the idea that certain traits of human behavior—including intelligence—were dictated by bodily fluids, also called the "humors" of the body. His theories were widely accepted throughout the Middle Ages, which ended after the fifth century A.D. (See chapter 4 for a more detailed discussion of Galen's theories.)

Sir Francis Galton, a 19th-century British scientist, is credited with developing some of the first tests for intelligence. He reportedly believed that certain families were biologically superior to others and that these traits were passed on from one generation to the next. The early tests that Galton developed in the late 1800s included rough measurements of the size of a subject's head, lung capacity, and grip strength—factors that we now know have no bearing on an individual's intelligence.

Galton is credited with making many contributions to psychology, including the development of what some consider the first psychological questionnaire, the use of the first statistical correlation, and the association of childhood experiences with adult behavior. And apparently Galton's beliefs about intelligence were not entirely wrong after all. Although modern research into this area continues, it now appears that intelligence is, in fact, derived from both heredity and environment.

THE IQ TEST

In more recent times, researchers have developed better ways to measure intelligence. At the beginning of the 20th century, French psychologists Alfred Binet and Theodore Simon developed an intelligence quotient formula, the forerunner of the modern IQ tests.

Around 1904, school attendance became compulsory in France. Before that time children who were considered slow learners had been kept at home. The French government commissioned Binet and Simon to come up with a way to identify which schoolchildren could learn from the standard curriculum in the country's schools and which could not.

Faced with this monumental task, the two psychologists reasoned that some children's mental abilities were simply more advanced than others. In other words, they assumed that those who performed well on academic material had the capabilities of older children and that those who performed poorly were not "dull" but merely normal for younger children. This led Binet and Simon to develop the concept of "mental age." They established a scale of what would be considered normal mental abilities for children through each stage of development and used the scale to determine each child's "mental age." These criteria included concepts and abilities that a majority of children at a particular age generally understood or exhibited.

Binet first published this scale in 1905, and it was later refined and revised. In 1916 Lewis Terman at Stanford University produced one of the most widely used revisions. Designed for use on children in the United States, this version of the scale—which has been revised several times—became commonly known as the Stanford-Binet test. At the suggestion of German psychologist William Stern, Terman coined the

At the beginning of the 20th century, school attendance became compulsory in France, and the French government commissioned Alfred Binet and Theodore Simon to determine how to identify schoolchildren who would be able to learn from the standard curriculum. The result was the development of a mathematical equation for what is now known as IQ.

concept of an "intelligence quotient," now commonly known as "IQ." The formula for finding a child's intelligence quotient looks like this:

$$IQ = (\text{Mental Age} \div \text{Chronological Age}) \times 100$$

Divide the subject's mental age by his or her chronological age and multiply the result by 100 to calculate the IQ.

Why multiply the result by 100? Numerous sources indicate that this particular multiplier was selected to represent an "average" score when a subject's mental age is equal to his or her chronological age. In other words, if a 10-year-old subject has a mental age of exactly 10, then the intelligence quotient for that child would be 100 (10 divided by 10 equals 1, which, multiplied by 100, equals 100). This proves beneficial for quickly measuring a subject's abilities in terms of below-average, average, or above-average ranking. A subject with a mental age lower than his or her chronological age would score below 100, whereas someone with a mental age higher than his or her chronological age would score above 100.

CURVING THE RESULTS

Common results of such tests as the Stanford-Binet are often fairly predictable among groups. Statistical odds indicate that about 46 to 50 percent of a group will produce average scores between 90 and 109. Low-average scores range from 80 to 89, and high-average results fall between 110 and 119; both of these ranges represent about 16 percent of the group as a whole.

The next step up is the range of scores between 120 and 139, which is considered "superior" and represents about 6–11 percent of most groups. Scores on the other end of the scale, which are called "borderline," are those between 70 and 79, also roughly 6–11 percent of most groups.

Subjects who score below 70 are considered "mentally retarded"; statistical projections estimate that about 2–3 percent of the subjects in a given test group will fall within this category. About 1–2 percent of a group is expected to score in the "very superior" range—higher than 139.

These predictions are derived from analysis of actual results—the norms we discussed in chapter 1. When these results are shown in a graphic format, such as a chart, they produce a bell-shaped curve, aptly known as a "bell curve" (see the figure below).

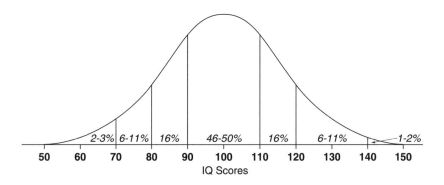

This shape is produced because the highest number of subjects score in the average, or middle, range. From there, numbers drop nearly symmetrically on both sides, with the lowest figures found at the two extremes.

GROWING PAINS

One problem that arose in the development of intelligence testing was how to deal with the changes in scores that occurred as children grew up. As the chronological ages of subjects progressed, many reached the upper limits of their mental abilities. This meant that at some point, subjects' mental ages would slow or cease to advance. Chronological ages, however, do not slow. Without an adjustment to the formula, children would eventually appear to be losing intelligence. As a result, the scores were adjusted. Some critics contended that this action stripped the formula of its true mathematical sense of producing a "quotient." There were other problems as well. Later studies showed that environmental circumstances such as where and how children were raised and such factors as language and ethnic differences affected the results. Critics argued that a cultural bias inherent in the test discriminated against less-privileged racial, ethnic, and social groups. Some of these controversies remain unresolved, and psychologists continue to work to create more effective tests.

TESTING ADULTS

In 1955 Dr. David Wechsler of Bellevue Psychiatric Hospital in New York City developed a new test—the Wechsler Adult Intelligence Scale, or WAIS—specifically for assessing adult intelligence.

Like the Stanford-Binet IQ test, WAIS was designed to be administered one-on-one by a battery of experienced testers. Among its other similarities to the Stanford-Binet test was its use of a series of subtests to measure performances that could be converted into a single IQ score. However, instead of basing these subtests on age ranges, WAIS grouped them into two different categories—"verbal" and "performance" abilities.

The verbal subtests assessed knowledge of information, general comprehension, memory span, arithmetic reasoning, ability to identify similarities, and vocabulary. Subtests in the performance category included picture arrangement, picture completion, block design, and object assembly. Results from the subtests could be scored individually to allow for comparison among a subject's individual abilities.

Both the verbal and performance categories could be assigned an individual score as well. This allowed for some latitude in ranking the mental abilities of adults. Instead of providing one all-encompassing score to rate an individual, psychologists could now examine a subject's abilities in terms of strengths and weaknesses.

OTHER WECHSLER TESTS

In addition to WAIS, Wechsler produced two tests for children: the Wechsler Intelligence Scale for Children (WISC), which was designed for children between ages 6 and 16, and the Wechsler Preschool and Primary Scale of Intelligence (WPPI), which was geared toward children between ages 4 and $6^1/_2$. These tests included the same principles found in the WAIS test. They clearly displayed the advantage to Wechsler's assertion that "intelligence is the aggregate or global capacity of the individual to act purposefully, to think rationally and to deal effectively with his environment."

Although Binet and Wechsler apparently agreed that a variety of test items were needed in order to measure the many demonstrable abilities that constitute intelligence, Binet believed that the nature of these abilities changes with age. In the pursuit of their goals, both men created what were considered "individual" tests—designed to be administered to one person at a time.

But it's a crowded world. As the new millennium begins, the earth—having experienced a dramatic increase in population over the past 100 years—is now home to about 6 billion people. Now, more than ever, there is a need for intelligence tests that can be administered to many people at once.

TESTING FOR THE MASSES

The need to test large numbers of subjects simultaneously spawned the concept of group IQ tests. One example is the Army General Classification Test (AGCT). During World War II (1941–45), the army administered this newly developed test to millions of individuals. Administrators used the test to determine candidates for skilled and unskilled duties; to select those who would be likely to benefit from further training; and to identify individuals with below-average intelligence, who would be considered unfit for service.

One of many criticisms leveled against this test was that administrators often carried it out in an environment that was not conducive to

The SAT and ACT measure skills, rather than knowledge, acquired during primary and secondary school. This young woman is taking the SAT prior to application for admission to various colleges and universities.

proper testing—including crowded, noisy, and confusing conditions. Further, the test reportedly had numerous cultural biases. A high failure rate resulted, which led some people to draw the erroneous conclusion that a high proportion of military recruits were of below-average intellect.

Since the time of the AGCT, however, branches of the military of the United States and other nations have adopted many other tests in order to better evaluate applicants in terms of both approval for service and assignment to particular duties.

Other commonly known group tests include the Scholastic Assessment Test (SAT) and the American College Test (ACT), which are considered in determining whether a student will be admitted to a particular college or university. These tests do not examine subjects' current knowledge of specific topics and fields of study. The tests focus on the subjects' abilities to use the skills that they have acquired during their 12 years of elementary and secondary education in order to solve new problems. It is virtually impossible to gain admittance to a U.S. institution of higher learning without taking at least one of these two tests.

CONCERNS

Some concerns about the stigma of psychological testing are unfounded. However, problems with group and individual intelligence tests do exist. Among the valid concerns are invasion of privacy, emotional trauma to the subjects, and the possibility that misuse of results will engender unfairness to certain groups or individuals.

Concerns over invasion of privacy are minimized when the purpose of the test in question is of little consequence. For example, a classroom of six-year-olds may undergo testing on their preferences between one book and another to determine potential curriculum changes. In this case the test may be viewed as helpful for development of educational programs rather than as a probe into the psyche of young children. However, if those same children undergo testing for traits and tendencies in more volatile areas—such as ethnic or racial preferences, moral values, or feelings toward family members—social outcry may follow.

Similarly, if tests are administered with little or no clear explanation of what their purpose is and what will be done with the results, this can emotionally traumatize children and adults. For example, a subject may become very anxious about the possibility that a test may reveal a severe problem. Or an individual may experience great concern that he or she will suffer embarrassment, or even perhaps the loss of a job, if results of the test fall into the hands of unauthorized persons. Administrators must take great care to explain tests clearly and honestly to subjects (and their parents, if the subjects are children) if they hope to prevent reactions ranging anywhere from simple anxiety over the inaccuracy of results to emotional damage and lawsuits.

In the same way, a child's low score on an IQ test given in a school setting should cause no more trauma than low scores on his or her schoolwork may already be producing. The IQ test might actually assist educators in identifying the student's particular problems in comprehending the material presented and may help them suggest some course of corrective action.

Still, in an age of increasing technological capabilities, where data storage and the security of that information is open to question, it is understandable that some subjects (or their parents) might express con-

DIFFERENCES IN MINORITY TESTING

For years, U.S. psychologists have debated why African Americans as a group consistently score lower on IQ tests than Caucasian Americans do. But psychologists have proposed no satisfactory explanation that can be supported with empirical data. In 1978 and 1994, however, John Ogbu published works suggesting that we might find the answer more easily if we also studied disadvantaged groups around the world.

He found that, like African Americans, the Maori in New Zealand, the "untouchables" in India, non-European Jews in Israel, and the Burakumin in Japan could all be described as "involuntary minorities." Unlike "voluntary minorities," such as immigrant groups who came to the United States in search of a better life, involuntary minorities had no choice about their place in their respective societies. They were forced into slavery or into other demeaning roles.

Ogbu discovered that, all over the world, children of involuntary minorities do not perform as well in school as does the majority population and that they drop out of school sooner. Their test scores are usually lower.

Ogbu has suggested that children of involuntary minorities grow up firmly convinced that their life will eventually be restricted to a poorly rewarded set of social roles. He theorizes that, because of this, these children lack what he terms "effort optimism"–the belief that hard work and serious commitment, particularly in school, will be rewarded.

The degree to which such attitudes are responsible for African-American test scores and academic achievement has not been established through objective

cern about who has access to test results. Students and their parents have a right to know what potential for harm could arise from unauthorized access to test results.

Subjects may become stigmatized (shamed or discredited) by the comparison of their results to those of other people taking the same test. Subjects with "average" scores could be unfairly denied access to accelerated programs and other beneficial experiences if some aspect of the

In our ethnically diverse society, it is important to consider how outside factors can affect minority testing. John Ogbu has suggested, for example, that the status of involuntary minorities discourages "effort optimism."

tests. However, addressing the question from an international perspective may introduce approaches to the issue that deserve further research.

(Adapted from "Intelligence: Knowns and Unknowns," report of a task force established by the Board of Scientific Affairs of the American Psychological Association, Washington, D.C., August 7, 1995.)

administration of the test caused them to perform below their abilities. If, for similar reasons, average students score below average, they could be unjustly categorized as low in intelligence or "mentally retarded." Conversely, average subjects might achieve higher scores than their actual capabilities should indicate. This could result in their being placed in programs that are beyond their ability to complete.

Finally, controversy has raged for decades over whether some tests might discriminate against certain groups or individuals. Some people have used test results to claim that certain minority groups are inherently more or less intelligent. In many such cases, however, such factors as environment, language, and test bias have proven to play a highly significant role in the discrepancies among the scores of the various groups of subjects.

One of the best methods is to use intelligence tests in conjunction with other criteria when assessing the intelligence of subjects. No one test has proven to be consistently accurate and conclusive in making such determinations.

HOW MUCH FAITH SHOULD WE PLACE IN TESTS?

The 19th-century British naturalist Charles Darwin stated, "If the misery of our poor be caused not by the laws of nature, but by our institutions, great is our sin."

In his 1981 book *The Mismeasure of Man*, author Stephen Jay Gould took a critical look at what he called a human urge to classify people according to their abilities and limits. He examined this tendency from the time when those gifts were considered to be divine allocations to the time when a numerical measurement could define nearly every aspect of human behavior.

Noting the fallacies of past practices, such as measuring the size of a person's cranium to predict intelligence, Gould pointed to the taint on the objectivity of science when it is performed as a social act that reflects the norms of the society in which it is conducted. He also contended that the science of testing can be colored, and thus rendered less accurate, by the scientists' own prejudices and personalities.

More specifically, though, Gould asserted that, despite the merits of the intentions, Binet's work—and subsequently Terman's mass marketing of intelligence testing and the U.S. Army's use of psychological testing—has been misrepresented in the United States. This misrepresentation, Gould asserted, has led to "subtle, mistaken and all-pervading judgement of races, classes and sexes; it is a theory of limits whose essence is that differences among people arise mostly from genetic inheritance, that biology is destiny."

Gould and many others contend that too great a reliance on intelligence testing can lead to false assumptions about individuals and groups of people. When society places too much faith in testing, it fails to consider all relevant aspects of human behavior. Some of the assumptions that people make as a result of intelligence testing can and do influence the way members of a society view others and themselves. These assumptions must be treated with the utmost care; they must be placed in contexts in which other factors will demonstrate or disprove their validity.

It is important to note that, although it is likely that such sources as political, social, and economic factors have engendered many of the controversies that we continue to debate as a society, twisting scientific data to support or refute social concerns is a precarious tactic, at best.

The next chapter looks at testing for a characteristic that can influence how we perceive others and how others perceive us in terms of intelligence—personality.

The second-century Greek physician Galen believed that bodily fluids were primarily responsible for personality. He associated black bile with melancholy—a general feeling of depression and unhappiness—depicted here by German artist Albrecht Dürer.

4

TESTING FOR PERSONALITY

The common expression "He [or she] has a great personality" is somewhat flawed. *Great* is a relative term, and it is open to interpretation. What one person would describe as a great personality another person may not.

Technically, personality is not something that a person has. Rather, the term describes certain characteristics of an individual's behavior. *Personality* is commonly defined as the distinctive way that each person thinks, feels, behaves, or adapts to various situations.

Over the years, there have been numerous definitions of *personality*. According to psychologist Raymond B. Cattell, personality is something that will allow us to predict what a person will do in a given situation. Psychologist Gordon Allport defined the term as the dynamic organization of a person's physical and psychological systems that determine how he or she will adjust to certain surroundings. Similarly, the German-born British psychologist Hans Jürgen Eysenck described personality as "a more stable and enduring organization" of an individual's characteristics as they relate to the way he or she adapts to various environments.

The list of definitions goes on, with each explanation varying slightly but remaining more or less true to several core elements. Whether psychologists talk about prediction, predisposition, or individual differences—or even common, measurable traits—they define *personality* as the way a person views his or her own thoughts, feelings, and behaviors and those of others and the way those thoughts, feelings, and behaviors help the person adapt to various environments and circumstances.

PERSONAL MASKS

Personality is derived from the Latin word *persona*, which means "mask." We might think of an individual's personality as the mask that he or she wears for others or as the way that others see him or her. We could also identify these characteristics as the mask a person wears to see him- or herself, as well as the way the individual views other people. Depending upon how technical we want to be, these characteristics could all be part of one grand mask for others and for the individual, or they could be many interchangeable masks to be worn at different times, among different people, or in different situations.

Personality and intelligence are interrelated. Among the ways in which they differ from each other, however, is the following: whereas a person's intelligence may remain constant in any given situation, his or her personality—how the individual feels, thinks, and behaves—is more likely to change. Other differences between personality and intelligence become clearer as we examine how methods of testing for personality have developed and progressed over the years.

EARLY THEORIES OF PERSONALITY TESTING

Just as there are many definitions of *personality*, there are many theories about the best method of determining an individual's personality. Some of these theories and methods may seem ludicrous by today's standards, yet elements of each are in use in modern society.

To explore some of the prevalent early theories, we must once again refer to Galen, the second-century Greek physician who associated various human behaviors with the bodily fluids, or "humors." Under Galen's theory, four humors were primarily responsible for human personality: blood, phlegm, yellow bile (urine), and black bile (stool). He applied his theory according to which of the fluids played the largest role in dictating a person's actions.

People whose bodies produced a greater amount of phlegm than considered normal in the general populace were labeled "phlegmatic" under Galen's theory. He interpreted the personality of phlegmatic people to be detached, aloof, unemotional, and uninvolved. Galen based this interpretation on his perception that phlegm itself was cold, moist, and unmoving; the phlegmatic people that he identified could have been either calm, quiet, and uninvolved or just plain slow or dull.

People that Galen identified as having blood as the primary humor received a slightly better profile. Those who were "driven by their blood," Galen proposed, were hearty, outgoing types who were robust, uninhibited, and optimistic. These sanguine people, as he also called them, were cheerful and tended to enjoy physical pleasures.

Galen identified those people who were most influenced by yellow and black biles—which he believed to be produced by the liver—as having much less desirable traits. He associated angry, ill-tempered, hateful people with the yellow bile, and he believed that black bile caused people to become melancholy. Symbolic of death to Galen, black bile induced depression, unhappiness, and even suicidal tendencies.

Under Galen's theory, the biological tendencies of a person determined his or her personality type—sanguine (blood), phlegmatic (phlegm), choleric (yellow bile), or melancholic (black bile)—and the type determined the person's various traits.

THEORIES TAKE SHAPE

Variations of Galen's theory of personality as based on the four humors continued throughout the centuries. But as modern psychology began to develop in the late 19th and early 20th centuries, new ideas about personality emerged.

Many people consider Sigmund Freud (1856–1939) to be the originator of modern psychology. He developed theories about personality based on lengthy and repeated interviews, primarily with wealthy European women.

Freud believed that sometimes what motivates a person is an undetected, deeply buried emotion or idea. Even the individual is unaware of what is driving his or her actions. Freud called the part of a person's mental ability that lies beyond conscious control or awareness the *unconscious.*

Freud also devised a theory that gave a structure to personality. He called the unconscious, or instinctual, component the "id." The id, he contended, contains an individual's inherited impulses, which crave immediate gratification. He called the energy that fuels these desires the "libido." The pleasure principle is the id being driven by the libido. The increase in the forces of a person's environment impose limitations on his or her efforts to gratify the id. A second component of personality then begins to emerge—the "ego."

Deriving its energy from the id, the ego resides partly in the unconscious and partly in the conscious mind. Freud proposed that, as such, the ego has a connection to, or grasp of, the external forces of the environment. The ego's job is to find ways to facilitate the id's pursuit of pleasure without getting into trouble in the larger society. Because the ego has a connection to external realities, it operates on the reality prin-

Sigmund Freud, the father of modern psychology, developed a model of personality consisting of three components: the id, the ego, and the superego. His ideas, though controversial, influence personality theory and testing even today.

ciple. As you might guess, the pleasure and reality principles tend to remain in a state of conflict.

The third component of Freud's model of personality is the "superego." The superego contains the id and the ego, but it also transcends them. Its role in Freud's model is to internalize what the individual learns from the environment—such as laws, ethics, and moral values—and guide the id and the ego to a stable coexistence. The superego is like an internal referee. It knows all the rules, as well as the penalties for breaking them, and maintains order between the id and the ego so that the person is able to function.

Freud continued to test and revise his theories during his lifetime. In part because he observed people who shared many cultural, social, economic, and ethnic similarities, Freud's ideas—which may thus not apply to a more diverse population—remain controversial. Still, they continue to influence personality theory and testing today.

In the 1940s, Harvard scientist W. H. Sheldon offered a different theory. He asserted that people with certain bodily characteristics were predisposed to certain personalities. Sheldon's theory was based on "morphologies." This theory classified people according to three major body types: endomorphs, mesomorphs, and ectomorphs. Endomorphs were short, plump people, who tended toward obesity. Mesomorphs were muscular, athletic people with propensities for physical activity. Ectomorphs were tall, thin people who were prone to engage in more cerebral endeavors.

According to Sheldon, endomorphs tended to be lazy and talkative. They were fond of relaxing and socializing. Mesomorphs, he claimed, were energetic and assertive by nature. They craved competition and power. Finally, Sheldon considered ectomorphs to be naturally introverted. They preferred solitude to company and were intellectual but inhibited.

Of course, when Sheldon applied this theory to actual study subjects, he quickly determined that most people didn't fit easily into any one of the three categories. Instead, they tended to possess various aspects of each. Thus, Sheldon fine-tuned his theory. He developed a seven-point scale to reflect the gradations of each body type and then conducted further research on this modified version of his theory. Subsequent research supported some of Sheldon's findings; however, critics took a dim view of the failure of the approach to protect against testing bias and to account for such factors as age or cultural, social, and economic conditions.

TRAITS DEVELOP

Though bodily fluids and structures failed to explain definitively why certain types of people feel, think, and act in certain ways, they paved the way for the identification of certain common *traits* to explain the results of personality observations. The development of these trait theories emerged from the idea that certain predispositions, whether inherited or learned, produced certain general predictable results among a variety of conditions or circumstances. In other words, people could generally be expected to act, think, or feel a certain way if they possessed certain common, measurable traits.

Gordon Allport, who became a professor of psychology at Harvard University in 1930, was one of the first psychologists to take this approach. Over the next 37 years, he published major works about both personality and the analysis of prejudice. He theorized that people develop personal traits, or "dispositions."

Allport believed that each individual has unique traits. He organized these traits into three main categories: central, secondary, and cardinal. Central traits make up the building blocks of an individual's personality. Terms such as *grumpy, smart, shy,* and *outgoing* refer to typical traits. Allport believed that most people have somewhere between 5 and 10 central traits. Secondary traits are not as obvious or as consistent. They reflect preferences and attitudes. "She gets angry when you tease her" describes a secondary trait. Allport believed that most or all individuals possess central and secondary traits but that only a select few possess cardinal traits. Cardinal traits are the traits that define a person's life. The fictional character Scrooge had the cardinal trait of greed. Mother Teresa spent her life motivated by religious service. Allport taught that people who have cardinal traits usually develop them later in life.

One major problem with Allport's theories was determining which among the multitude of perceived traits applied to which category. People often have different interpretations of words used to describe traits. And because Allport believed that each person's traits are unique, it was difficult to devise an objective way of testing for these characteristics.

At about the same time that Allport was developing his theories, Raymond B. Cattell put forth the idea that traits are inferred from an individual's actions. An observer might identify as independent a person who dresses in a unique way, regularly expresses his or her opinions, and doesn't join groups. Through research, Cattell identified 35 trait clusters. These are groups of traits that tend to go together, such as assertiveness, aggressiveness, and competitiveness. Because these clusters are based on external actions, Cattell labeled them "surface" traits.

Cattell later pared down these clusters to 16 "source" traits that iden-

Psychologist Gordon Allport developed a theory of personal traits, which he organized into three categories: central, secondary, and cardinal. In Charles Dickens's A Christmas Carol, *the character Scrooge displayed the cardinal trait of greed.*

tified more basic elements of personality. Then, in 1964, he developed a test that produced a profile of characteristics that a person might possess. Cattell noted that these characteristics might be produced by environmental or inherited factors.

Criticisms of this approach included the fact that Cattell's methods of gathering data and his focus on adults did little to illustrate how traits develop during childhood. Critics alleged that Cattell relied on erroneous or flawed sources for information, including personal records, reports from friends and relatives, and self-assessment.

Reports from others, they asserted, might not accurately describe an individual. For example, how many times have you heard the mystified neighbors of a man who has committed a horrendous act of violence tell television news reporters, "He was always such a quiet, friendly person"?

Self-assessments can be equally flawed, critics contended. People describing themselves are not likely to predict honestly how they might react in certain situations, or they may not really know how they might react until they actually face a situation.

Perhaps the most general criticism of Cattell's approach was the argument that thoughts and behaviors are not directly determined by someone's personality; they are determined by how the characteristics that people possess blend with their current environment. People's characteristics may change as their lives change. The criticisms aside, however, Cattell developed a fairly comprehensive way to measure some of the traits that motivate people's actions.

Hans Jürgen Eysenck took the field a step further by developing a theory and model that examines "normal" and "abnormal" personality traits in terms of three basic dimensions. His studies leaned more toward the notion that learning and personality traits may be determined by genetic, rather than environmental, factors.

Critics took exception with Eysenck's theories, often citing the same arguments that had been used against Cattell. Eysenck's approach became the subject of even greater controversy after he suggested that genetic makeup may be responsible for IQ differences between white people and black people.

In general, critics of trait or dispositional theories pointed out that these methods offered little determination of how personality develops or changes. For that, they turned to psychoanalytic theories, which built upon the earlier work of Freud.

PSYCHOANALYTIC THEORIES

Carl Jung and Alfred Adler were among those who built upon Freud's work with the unconscious mind and its effect on personality development.

Jung worked with Freud for several years, but they parted ways because they could not agree on several important aspects of personality theory. Jung divided people into two groups. *Extroverts* looked outward and used social interaction as a way to live out their inner drives.

Introverts looked to their inner world, sometimes at the expense of social interaction. Jung also theorized that everyone shares a collective unconscious and possesses instinctive patterns that he called "archetypes." Jung pioneered the use of psychotherapy among the middle-aged and elderly, helping them use their dreams and imagination to discover new beliefs to replace earlier beliefs that they had discarded.

Adler, who studied under Freud, also parted ways with him. He became known for developing a system of individual psychology with an emphasis on a holistic approach to human problems, in which he considered the whole person in his or her interactions with the environment. Adler taught that most people strive toward completeness. Feelings of inferiority, inadequacy, or incompleteness caused by a number of factors—physical defects, economic status, treatment during childhood—frustrate the journey toward completeness. A mentally healthy individual, Adler maintained, compensates for feelings of inferiority by developing his or her abilities and working for the common good. A person who is not as healthy, however, may develop an *inferiority complex,* in which his or her personality revolves around attempts to make up for some perceived deficiency or lack. This can manifest itself as an egocentric drive for power or as concern about oneself at the expense of others. Followers of Adler's approach help a patient recognize his or her unsuccessful methods of coping with feelings of inferiority. Then they help the individual build up self-esteem, adopt more realistic goals, and develop more concern for the well-being of the larger society.

Many aspects of psychoanalytic personality theories are now generally accepted. However, these theories are based on information that psychologists obtain by listening to their patients' stories. The theories do not allow for independent observation or repeated testing. But they do point out the need for personality testing to go beyond simple description of types of people. Psychologists eventually realized that it was necessary to develop repeatable scientific tests that would quantify how people become who they are and how they change.

TESTS

As we have seen, personality tests seek to determine the various traits that make individuals unique, common, or somewhere in between. In chapter 2 we learned that these kinds of tests are generally divided into two major categories—objective tests and projective tests. If psychologists are to determine personality development as well as personality traits, both types of tests are needed.

PROJECTIVE PERSONALITY TESTS

In 1911, Hermann Rorschach developed a classic example of the projective personality test. The Rorschach Inkblot Test consists of 10 printed shapes that the administrator shows to a subject one at a time in a specified order. The tester asks the subject to describe what he or she sees in the shapes—much the way a person might identify shapes in the clouds on a beautiful spring afternoon.

The administrator records not only the subject's responses but also his or her mannerisms, expressions, and other behaviors during the test. The tester then analyzes and compiles all of these observations and the test responses to formulate a basic (not complete) psychological profile of the subject.

Of course, the primary criticism of such a projective test is its subjective nature. Although it may purport to allow a glimpse into the subject's unconscious, the possibility exists that the administrator may unconsciously introduce his or her own personality into the interpretation of the results. In addition, these tests lack definitiveness, leaving the results as open to interpretation as are the responses of the subjects. The Rorschach test has proven useful when administered skillfully; however, because of its subjective nature, it has a low level of reliability and validity. Other criticisms include the considerable time and other resources the test can require to administer.

Efforts to develop more comprehensive scoring systems and improve standardization and norms for the test have thus far proven largely unsuccessful. The Holtzman Inkblot Test, involving 45 inkblots, attempted to eliminate some of the statistical problems present in the Rorschach test. Research continues on how useful these tests are in comparing psychiatric patients and other special groups to the "normal" population.

The Thematic Apperception Test (TAT) is a projective test that does not use inkblots. The TAT uses a series of 30 simple black-and-white pictures and a blank card. The pictures show people involved in various activities, such as playing a musical instrument. The tester presents the subject with each card and asks him or her to make up a story based on the image. The vague, ambiguous nature of the images is designed to make the subject project his or her inner conflicts onto the resulting stories. The blank card offers a way to test the subject's imagination when very little stimulation is provided. Psychologists often use the analysis to determine conscious and unconscious needs that they infer from each subject's stories.

Critics find fault with the TAT, as they do with the inkblot tests, for the subjective nature of the test and for the time and expense involved in administering the test and interpreting its results. As is the case with many projective tests, the reliability of the TAT depends primarily on the ability of the tester to refrain—if it is humanly possible to do so—from introducing his or her own personality traits into the analysis.

OBJECTIVE PERSONALITY TESTS

Objective personality tests have the advantage of being somewhat more structured than projective tests. One of the most popular is the Minnesota Multiphasic Personality Inventory, or MMPI. Developed in the 1940s, the MMPI is reportedly the most widely used personality test in the United States for clinical assessment and research. Internationally, the MMPI has been translated into more than 115 languages and has been used in nearly 50 countries.

The MMPI is used extensively for clinical personality testing and research in the United States. Here an expert explains the test during a 1999 murder trial in Florida.

Personality tests provide information that can prove helpful during family counseling. For example, personality testing might help this mother and father gain insight into their parenting styles.

The development of the MMPI came about through administration of the test to a large group of "normal" individuals, as well as to groups of psychiatric patients. Analysis of the results enabled experts to establish clinical scales. These scales measure for various personality disorders, such as depression and mania. Testers compare a subject's results with the results of a group of individuals known to be depressed.

The MMPI uses a *self-reporting technique*, in which subjects provide information about themselves. One version of the test includes 550 "true or false" questions. The MMPI also includes questions that assess a subject's tendencies to skew the test results. These validity scales measure inclinations toward defensiveness, carelessness, exaggeration, and other qualities that could affect the accuracy of the subject's responses. The scales help answer criticisms that inaccuracies in a subject's self-perception necessarily distort the results of self-reporting tests.

In 1989, researchers revised the MMPI and released it as the MMPI-2. They removed objectionable items, reworded some sections to make them better reflect contemporary language, and added new entries. Researchers restandardized the norms and scales based on a randomly selected national sample. The close attention that developers of the MMPI and the MMPI-2 paid to the issues of reliability and validity has contributed to the continued popularity of these tests among a variety of therapists. Although some opponents have labeled the tests superficial, dated, or too oriented toward measuring unobservable characteristics, the MMPI and MMPI-2 remain in wide use.

Over the years, researchers have developed a number of other fairly prominent tests to identify and gauge personality traits. (For a listing of some of these, see Appendix: Selected Psychological Tests.) These tests are helpful not only to psychologists and individuals who want to better understand personalities but also to individuals in marriage and family counseling settings.

Researchers have developed tests to aid in determining the compatibility of a couple contemplating marriage. There are tests that can identify, and thus help counselors address, differences in parenting styles. Some tests can give parents insight into the distinctions among their children. As family members increase their understanding of each other's personalities, they can determine more effective ways of resolving conflicts and working together.

Most children will demonstrate no need for individual psychological testing. Their families will watch them progress normally throughout childhood—in their development, in their learning, and in their interaction with others.

5

TESTING CHILDREN

Although many parents give accounts to the contrary, most children are of about average intelligence. Remember the bell curve in chapter 3? Testing is probably the most direct and accurate way of determining how intelligent a child may be. But to those parents who worry that their child may have some form of learning disability or other problem, which they seek to identify and correct, testing can be a source of great concern.

Most children do not need to be tested. They develop, learn, and interact with their surroundings quite normally, with no apparent cause for alarm. From infancy through toddlerhood and the preschool stages, they progress with thinking, reasoning, language, and other mental skills. They develop acceptable and even familiar emotional traits—even if not always in perfect harmony with their environment—as they transform themselves into distinct individuals.

For some children, however, problems can and do become apparent at some stage in their development. In these cases, if parents find that they are not as well equipped to deal with the situation as they would like to be, professional help may be needed. Testing is one method that psychologists may use to help identify a child's problems more accurately.

WHY TEST CHILDREN?

Previously we discussed some early psychological testing that probed various ways of identifying and classifying intelligence levels but failed to account for the development and growth of children. But a lot has changed since Binet first tested young schoolchildren in the early 1900s. Today, there are scores of psychological tests designed specifically for children—including various modern children's versions of the popular Wechsler and Stanford-Binet intelligence tests and the MMPI, TAT, and Rorschach personality tests. (For a listing

For some children, recurring behavioral problems may prompt a professional to recommend psychological testing. Here a junior high school principal discusses disruptive behavior with a student.

of some of the specific tests, with their corresponding age ranges, see Appendix: Selected Psychological Tests.)

There are many circumstances under which a professional may suggest that a particular child undergo psychological testing. An educator may recommend testing for a child who has shown signs of mental abilities beyond his or her age, in order to plan a special curriculum that will keep the child intellectually challenged. Conversely, a child who is performing below expected levels or who shows signs of some emotional problem may be an appropriate candidate for testing.

When someone reaches out to a child who is displaying signs of distress, instead of ignoring a situation that could worsen as time passes, the child frequently benefits from the effort. It is often easier to deal with problems during childhood than to try to reverse deeply rooted psychological patterns in adults. It is usually up to parents, guardians, or other adults in authority to put aside their own fears of what problems may be uncovered and take the initiative to do what's best for the child.

SHOULD A CHILD BE TESTED?

When we consider whether to have a child tested, it is important to understand that the goal is not to create problems where none exist. The behavior observed in the child may, in fact, be perfectly normal, or it may be simple enough to correct without using extensive testing to make a diagnosis.

It is just as important not to invent or exaggerate potential problems as it is not to ignore them. So how does a parent know what course to take? Typically, when a teacher or some other child-care professional recommends that parents have their child tested, the adviser can provide a reasonably solid explanation for having made the recommendation.

A school administrator may recommend testing for a student who demonstrates advanced abilities, in order to tailor the curriculum to his or her needs. These children are participating in a music enrichment program.

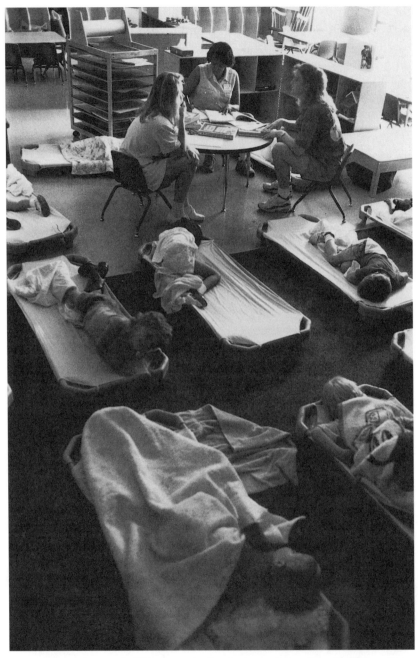

Parents frequently consult child-care professionals about whether they should have their children tested. Here preschool teachers offer advice to a concerned mother.

The best way for parents to determine whether testing is warranted is to consult with a child psychologist or other child-care professional, such as a teacher or a trained day-care provider, until all questions about the situation have been adequately addressed. These professionals often have considerable experience in identifying problems, and they may help to alleviate some concerns that the parents have about their child's behavior.

Another good way for parents to determine whether a child needs to be tested is to consult with the parents of other children to see whether they have observed similar traits or behaviors in their own children. Other parents who are dealing with children who exhibit comparable behaviors may recommend steps they have taken that have produced positive results.

Comparison can be beneficial to test developers and administrators in assimilating scores; however, it is not always an ideal way of rating and evaluating children to determine if they need special treatments or corrective measures. It may be helpful for parents to get opinions from psychologists or other professionals about whether their child would benefit from testing.

In most cases, discussing the situation with the child can prove beneficial as well. If it turns out that there is a problem that needs to be addressed, the next step is to consider whether testing will help. Is the purpose of testing truly the identification of a problem, or will the experience simply make the situation worse?

THE VALUE OF TESTING

A psychological test is merely a tool or an instrument used to help a child, but many psychologists have noted that being tested can itself actually induce very real anxieties and thus lead to other problems. These potential negative consequences must be weighed against the benefits that testing may provide. In most cases, if the perceived behavior problem seems severe enough to warrant consulting a psychologist in the first place, there is little reason to believe that a simple or complex test is going to cause or heighten the level of the child's anxiety. Still, it is a possibility that parents should consider.

Many parents wonder what value there is to testing a child when there are less-intrusive, personal ways to identify and correct problems. The trouble is that, by the time testing has been recommended, many

ONE GIRL'S STORY

Susan (as we will call her) tended to be quiet. Ever since she was a little girl, she had been extremely withdrawn. People would forget she was even around. When she did speak, she often called objects by the wrong names. In school, she hated reading and math because the letters, numbers, and symbols didn't make any sense to her. She had been told—and was convinced—that she was mentally retarded. She had very few friends.

When Susan entered sixth grade, she still couldn't do basic math. Her mother decided to take her to a private clinic for testing. During the assessment, the clinician observed that Susan had trouble connecting symbols with their meanings. This learning disability was causing her problems in language, reading, and math. But Susan scored 128 on an IQ test, indicating what is considered "superior" intelligence.

The clinician developed an individualized education plan for Susan and recommended that she receive counseling for her low self-esteem and depression.

Susan is now in ninth grade. She enjoys learning; has improved her speaking skills; and is making slow, steady progress in both math and reading. She loves making clothes and doll furniture for her little sister. Because of the way Susan's test results were used, her life has greatly improved and she is a happier person.

(Adapted from "Learning Disabilities," NIH Publication No. 93-3611, National Institutes of Health, Bethesda, Maryland, September 1993.)

parents may have tried these other methods with little or no success. Otherwise, the perceived problem would probably not warrant a referral from an outside source. Less-intrusive, personal methods of dealing with children's problems also tend to be subjective.

Parents who attempt to identify a problem in their child may overlook certain aspects of the child's behavior because they may perceive it as normal or because it is a behavior that the parents themselves display. Some behaviors that are acceptable in adults can be problematic for children. For example, adults should feel responsible for their children's well-being; however, when a child feels overly responsible for his or her brothers and sisters, a problem has developed.

Parents' affection for their children can also cause them to become oblivious to a child's problems. Sometimes it's easy to overlook negative behaviors in those we love. Parents of a girl who is unusually delayed in learning to talk may dismiss this by saying, "Jennifer is just a quiet child."

Psychological testing creates a more level playing field than parental observation by itself can provide. Lending objectivity to the equation, standardized tests can—without being overly harsh or cruel—reveal some of the allowances being made by parents. Tests simply delineate problems and allow the administrator to recommend a course of action to correct the situation. They do not inflict punishment or other disciplinary measures. Tests also serve to place children—to determine where they stand with their peers. Are they advanced, or are they lagging behind in academic performance? Are they feeling inadequate or alienated?

The most obvious value of testing is that it can gather the proper information that psychologists and parents need to make the best possible decisions for children. Testing attempts to minimize the amount of trial and error involved in working through a problem at a time when parents may need to make difficult decisions about their children.

PSYCHOLOGICAL ASSESSMENT

Because of the limitations of many individual psychological tests, they are sometimes administered in a battery format. This means that the psychologist will give the subject two or more tests in order to glean a different type of information from each. After administering the tests, the psychologist integrates and compiles data from the responses.

This battery of tests—which can also be accompanied by other tools, such as interviews with the subject and his or her family and friends; direct observation; and examination of school, medical, and other records—is known as a *psychological assessment*. Some of the records that may be consulted along with the tests are confidential, but they may contain information needed to make a proper psychological assessment. Parents control which of their child's records may be made available to the psychologist and which members of the child's immediate environ-

Parents' love for their children can sometimes cause them to overlook, or make excuses for, their children's behavior. In these situations, psychological tests can provide objectivity.

ment the psychologist may address when conducting interviews. Depending on the scope or severity of the problem, the parents may reduce or expand the amount of leeway that they give the psychologist in making the assessment. If a problem is severe, parents may be willing to increase the scope of data that they allow the psychologist to use. In most cases, the more information the parents make available, the more accurate the assessment will be. It is important to remember that a professional psychologist uses these tests to work for and with the parents in order to meet the needs of the child.

THE LAST WORD

It is critical to remember that parents usually have the final say in matters of psychological testing and treatment of children, except, of course, if a court order is involved or the parent or guardian represents some danger to the child. In such extreme cases, the issue of record confidentiality may become a matter for attorneys or law enforcement officials to determine.

Generally, parents love and nurture their children, and they have the ultimate authority to determine what is best for them. They may or may not have much in the way of training in the fields of psychology or education, but parents typically spend more one-on-one time with their children than anyone else does. As a result, they are often best equipped to recognize the patterns of their children's behavior, their values, and the limits of their abilities.

Such input from parents is probably the most valued in reaching any conclusions about an individual child's behavior. That isn't to say that parents always can or should go it alone. But their insights can be of great assistance to a psychologist looking to properly diagnose and treat a child with some emotional or learning problem.

When a child is scheduled for testing, it is important for parents to ensure that the child will be tested properly. There are many factors to consider, not the least of which is whether the test is a valid measure of the perceived problem. It is also important to remember that, even when a child is too young to understand what is happening during testing, the experience may prove traumatic. When a child has sufficient mental capacity to know what is going on, the parents and the psychologist should agree on what to tell the child before the test is administered. In addition, the parents and psychologist should assure the child that the test is not something that is harmful and is not a negative reflection on the child.

For parents, it's a little more complicated. Some parents fear that psychological testing will label their child in negative ways or that it may reveal inadequacies in their skills as parents. They may worry that testing will determine that there is something seriously wrong with their child, a conclusion that they may be hesitant to accept. But the true goal of administering psychological tests to children should be to provide information to be used for the children's benefit—not to ferret out flaws or point fingers of blame.

Again, it is important to remember that not all psychological testing of children is performed to identify negative traits. Testing can also help children by determining the levels of their abilities and allowing parents and educators to better tailor the materials or environments through which these children learn.

JUST BETWEEN US

Whatever the purpose of the test, parents and their child test subjects are often justly concerned with who will have access to the results and what they might do with that information. In most cases, all parties can be assured that the results will remain confidential unless there is some imperative reason to divulge the information. For example, if a child is found to be a danger to others or to him- or herself, or if there is some element of danger to the child from another source, such as a parent, the tester will often release the results to the proper authorities. But the confidentiality of information obtained from the testing of a child—or, for that matter, an adult—should not be violated unless there is clear evidence of some element of harm or danger that will remain unchecked unless it is reported to the proper authorities.

Confidentiality is a professional and ethical standard. When children undergo testing, parents or legal guardians hold a right to the information obtained by the psychology professional. Release of that information is afforded limited protection under law. The parent or guardian and the psychology professional typically agree on the terms of what can and should be kept confidential.

The primary benefit of confidentiality—in addition to the assurance to parents that personal details about their children will not be made available to others without their consent—is that it builds trust. Establishing and maintaining trust between the professional, the parents, and children is an important part of the process of identifying and correcting psychological problems. Without trust, subjects may not respond truthfully to test questions and other components, which could lead to ineffective or deficient diagnoses.

CONCLUSION

Any number of problems may occur in children at some point during their physical, emotional, social, and intellectual development. If a psychological problem develops, it is important to remember that there are courses of action to take that can help. The myriad psychological tests and assessments that are available can assist in the attempt to provide a realistic portrayal of a child of any age within the context of how the child interacts within his or her individual environment. These tests and assessments can then help psychologists and parents formulate a plan for addressing the problem.

Colleges and universities use interest testing to help students select areas of concentration and career paths. This student is checking out the summer job market in his chosen field.

TESTING FOR INTERESTS AND EMPLOYMENT

Experts use psychological testing to help teenagers and adults better understand their interests and work habits so that they can pursue careers that will be personally satisfying. Colleges and universities make such tests available to their students so that they can more easily select their majors and identify careers that fit their skills. Human resource departments in many companies use these tests to screen job applicants, to evaluate the suitability of current employees for specific assignments, and to select candidates for promotion.

The field of modern interest testing was born in Pittsburgh, Pennsylvania, in the early 1900s. Edward K. Strong, a psychologist who taught at the Carnegie Institute of Technology from 1919 to 1923, is credited with having published the Strong Vocational Interest Blank (SVIB) in 1927. This pencil-and-paper survey consisted of more than 300 items designed to determine the occupational paths that subjects should follow.

Because Strong felt that women chose paths very different from those that men chose, he published a separate "women's version" of the test in 1933. Subsequent revisions of the SVIB in the 1960s abandoned these gender differences, and the tests were combined into the Strong-Campbell Interest Inventory (SCII).

Many testers have used a later version, the SVIB-SCII, to help people choose educational and occupational paths. Researchers have developed a number of other tests to determine people's vocational interests, including the Kruder Occupational Interest Survey (KOIS), the Career Assessment Inventory (CAI), and the Jackson Vocational Interest Survey (JVIS).

CHOOSING CAREERS

High schools, colleges, and universities make use of interest tests to help their students better determine what career paths they might choose.

There are multiple versions of some tests, such as the CAI. The Vocational Version of the CAI targets jobs that require a high school diploma or an associate degree from a community college. The Enhanced Version of the CAI focuses on careers requiring a degree from a four-year college. Results for interest tests show ratings on such scales as general themes (for example, is the subject more interested in artistic themes or investigative themes?), basic interests (for example, mechanical, science, social service, and performing and entertaining), and specific occupations.

Other tests, such as the Campbell Interest and Skill Survey (CISS), go even further. They measure more than just the subject's attraction to specific occupational fields. They also include scales that estimate the subject's confidence in his or her ability to perform such functions.

The information from these tests equips students to select areas of academic study that will build their skills and better prepare them for a variety of careers that they are likely to find personally fulfilling.

WHEN LIFE BRINGS CHANGE

Interest tests also assist people who are facing major life changes. People with well-established career paths sometimes encounter unexpected problems. Downsizing in response to company mergers or changing economic cycles may cause job layoffs. As a result of changes in consumer tastes or federal regulations that cause the shrinking of a particular industry, people may lose their positions. In the United States, workers employed by wood-products industries in the Pacific Northwest and by mining interests in the Southeast have experienced such job cuts. Some people are involved in accidents or contract illnesses that prevent them from continuing in the work for which they were trained.

When people experience such drastic life changes, they may have no idea what other type of work they are qualified for or interested in. In such cases, interest and skill tests can help them in the transition from their former line of work to one that they may have never before considered.

EVALUATING PROSPECTIVE EMPLOYEES

Future employees are not the only people who benefit from interest and skills tests. For years, employers have used a variety of psychological tests in an effort to hire qualified workers. The ability to predict perfor-

Employers frequently test job candidates for particular openings. This woman's company is testing her suitability for a specific assignment within the firm.

mance can be beneficial to both the employer and the prospective employee. It helps the job seeker better determine whether the position is a good match for his or her abilities, and it helps the person who is doing the hiring better understand the skills that the job seeker has to offer.

Some managers and human resources professionals find it difficult to "read" a person they don't know. They realize that, in the presence of a prospective employer, a person often makes an effort to appear to be a more attractive candidate for the job than he or she actually is. Interest and skills tests can serve to reinforce or temper first impressions. When employers use the tests in this way, however, they must critically examine the reliability and validity of the tests.

Tests for job candidates are plentiful. Both academic and commercial institutions regularly purchase them. There are hundreds of test publishers in the United States. They publish individual and group tests, as well as objective and projective tests, in varying formats. There are printed tests, computerized tests, and mechanical tests. They measure intelligence, aptitude, ability, achievement, interest, personality, and other characteristics. They also attempt to define skills in such fields as mechanics, language, mathematics, music, and art.

There has been some controversy over the use of interest tests by human resources professionals to select candidates for jobs. Proponents contend that this approach can facilitate the hiring of more suitable workers, whose job satisfaction will encourage them to stay with a company for a longer period of time. Opponents, who view the tests as biased and lacking in objectivity, contend that the tests unfairly eliminate skilled workers from consideration.

ADA AND WORKPLACE TESTING

In part because of these concerns about the unfair elimination of job candidates, the 1990 Americans with Disabilities Act (ADA) changed testing in the workplace. With the passing of the ADA, it became illegal for employers to use medical tests (which can include psychological tests) or to ask questions about alcohol and drug use and psychiatric history in their assessment of potential employees. The intent of the law is to prevent employers from eliminating job candidates simply because they have mental or physical disabilities. The ADA is designed to encourage employers to examine the qualifications of each prospective employee, regardless of any disability that the individual may have.

This does not mean, however, that job applicants are free from taking all personality tests. The Equal Employment Opportunity Commission released ADA guidelines on medical examinations in October 1995. These guidelines allow testing if a test "is designed and used to measure only things such as honesty, tastes and habits."

But many tests designed primarily to identify personality traits can be used to diagnose personality disorders as well. This could conceiv-

With the passage of the Americans with Disabilities Act, disabled job candidates—such as this student at Middle Tennessee State University—are protected from being eliminated from consideration for employment based solely on their mental or physical disabilities.

ably leave test publishers and administrators open to lawsuits. Some psychologists and publishers continue to try to provide tests for job applicants. Other publishers have modified their tests. Consulting Psychologists Press, which publishes the California Personality Inventory, deleted 28 potentially problematic questions from the test.

Regularly scheduled personality tests are often required for people who hold positions of responsibility for the safety of others. Air traffic controllers, such as the one shown here, and other such professionals are tested periodically to determine their ability to handle day-to-day stress.

Many psychologists and test publishers—including the University of Minnesota Press, which publishes the MMPI—will not administer psychological tests to a person being considered for employment until after the individual has been offered a job. Until the courts decide which tests can be administered to job applicants without violating the ADA, many more psychologists and test publishers are likely to follow suit.

PUTTING TESTS TO WORK

In certain professions, psychological testing is clearly necessary in order to protect public safety. The hiring of law enforcement officers, emergency response workers, air traffic controllers, and other professionals who hold positions of responsibility for the well-being of others requires a special level of care. In addition, it is essential to take continual steps to ensure that the stresses of the job have not impaired the employee's ability to perform his or her duties.

For this reason, professionals such as airline pilots and police officers usually undergo regularly scheduled and required personality tests for as long as they hold their positions. Although tests cannot guarantee public safety, they can serve as a warning that an employee who is experiencing stress from work or outside factors is in need of help.

Many companies, no matter how great or small the stress created by their working environments may be, require their employees to take such tests as the Myers-Brigg Type Indicator. These tests help people better understand their own personalities, their working styles, and the working styles and personalities of their fellow employees. Proponents of this policy contend that such efforts improve the working environment and encourage employees to stay with a company for a long time.

Special situations, such as experiencing an assault on the job, may call for both professional counseling and psychological testing to help ensure that employees can work through the trauma of the event.

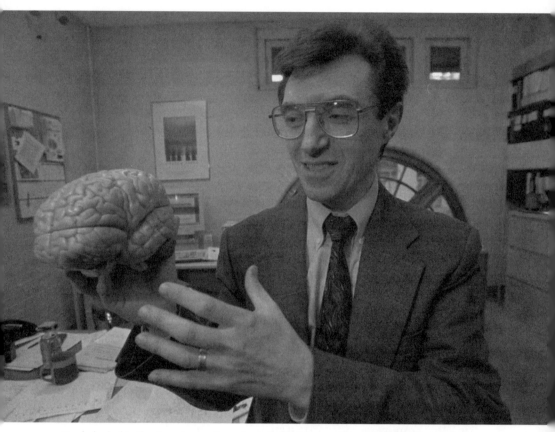

Psychological testing is no longer the only method of diagnosing mental disorders. Today neurological tests help psychologists identify these problems as well. Here Carnegie Mellon University researcher Marcel Just discusses the use of one such test, known as MRI.

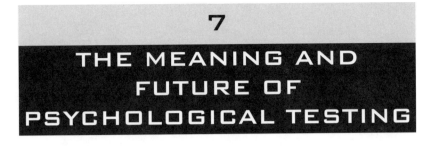

7

THE MEANING AND FUTURE OF PSYCHOLOGICAL TESTING

We have surveyed the last 100 years or so of the development of psycho-logical theories and the subsequent tests they have produced. We have also looked at the adaptation of these tests in the face of changing social structures and values. That leaves us with an obvious question: What do these tests mean? Simply put, they mean different things to different people.

As we have seen, various forms of intelligence and achievement tests, per-sonality and ability tests, and other types of psychological measurements are merely tools that psychologists may use to learn potentially important infor-mation about someone they are trying to help. Sometimes, one specific test is more than adequate to provide the data that a psychologist needs. Other times, several tests may be necessary to get to the root of the particular prob-lem being addressed or even to determine whether a problem actually exists. In order to conduct an assessment that will provide a more comprehensive picture than could any single test, a psychologist may administer multiple tests, perhaps combining them with the use of other tools, such as school and medical records or interviews with family and friends.

Whether one test or many are used, however, it falls to the psychologists to evaluate and interpret the resulting information, produce a diagnosis, and prescribe a proper method for treating the problem, if one exists. Thus, the question of what psychological tests mean is often as open to interpretation as are the results of any one test.

Psychological testing may also mean different things to different people. To some, the results of a test may be very important, providing a previously elu-sive answer that explains a particular pattern of behavior. Other people may not place any importance on testing, let alone on the results. These individuals may have no interest in exploring why they exhibit some peculiar pattern of behavior, or they may rationalize it through other means. They may offer a

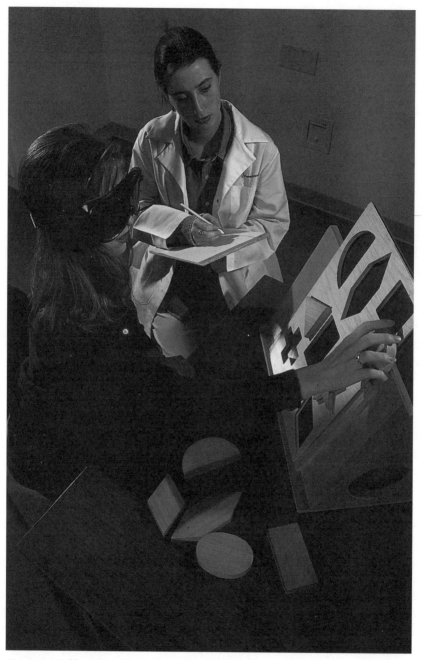

Here a mental health professional records results as she administers a psychological test. She will then evaluate and interpret the results in order to determine the problem and recommend treatment.

variety of explanations, such as "That's the way I am" or "Our family has always been like this."

Social and religious values, environment, culture, and even economic constraints can play a role in both determining what the results of a specific test or of an assessment may indicate and shaping what these results will mean to the subjects. Test subjects may learn something beneficial about themselves, have that information reinforced by test results, and simply choose to disbelieve or ignore it. They may even contend that the tests have no actual bearing on their day-to-day, real-life situations.

Over the past 100 years, psychologists have faced considerable challenges in the development of methods of extracting information from people that will contribute to an understanding of what makes individuals behave in the ways they do. In previous chapters, we saw that since psychological testing began, criticisms have accompanied nearly all advancements in the field. Some of the objections were simply minor disagreements, having little to no effect on a test's acceptance; others virtually eliminated some theories from the body of accepted study.

In most cases, nonetheless, these studies, theories, and developments have shared one thing in common—they each attempted to address some particular aspect of human behavior in a way that would provide optimal solutions to understanding and measuring the aspects of that behavior. In light of the importance of the goal of testing methodology, the importance of criticizing any perceived flaws or lack of validity or reliability becomes clear.

The field of psychology continues to change. Current research is discovering that biological factors can contribute to or identify various mental illnesses. Research is also helping to clarify how the brain works and how learning takes place. Not too long ago, psychological testing was the only objective method available for diagnosing mental illnesses or projecting academic success. Medical discoveries have now added new technologies to the psychologist's array of tools, and they may well lead to new diagnostic medical tests in the future. Electroencephalograms (EEGs), computed tomographic scanning (CT scan), and positron emission tomography (PET) are among the neuropsychiatric tests currently being used to assist in some psychological diagnoses.

EEGs record and interpret the electrical activity of the brain. Developed in 1929, this test provides a way of studying how the brain works. It can detect irregular brain waves that come from localized areas of brain damage and is helpful in the diagnosis of serious head injuries, brain tumors and infections, epilepsy, and degenerative diseases of the nervous system, all of which can contribute to changes in behavior.

Medical personnel also use the CT scan to evaluate patients suspected of having brain tumors, subdural hematomas, or strokes that are affecting their behavior. Developed in the early 1970s, the CT scan provides cross-sectional x-ray images of the brain. Magnetic resonance imaging (MRI), which is usually better than the CT scan at revealing some brain lesions, is helpful in such situations as well.

PET scans determine the presence of various neurological abnormalities. Preliminary findings in patients with schizophrenia and bipolar disorder reveal that their brains show marked differences from the brains of "normal" subjects. PET scans can actually show the rate of blood flow from one area of the brain to another. Researchers are using PET scans to study the ways that different parts of the brain work when a subject engages in different types of activities. In addition, some research indicates that various hormone tests may become biological markers for mood disorders such as depression and panic disorder.

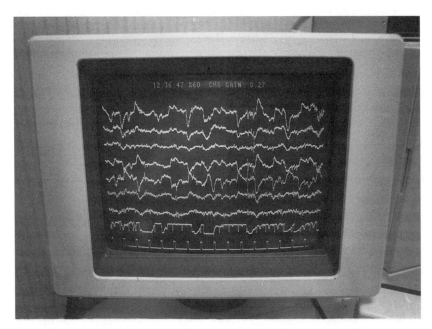

Medical researchers can gain much information about brain activity from EEGs, which record brain activity as lines such as the ones shown on this monitor.

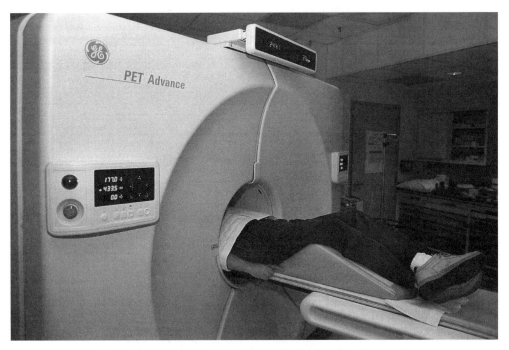

PET scans are used to diagnose a number of neurological disorders. The test, shown here in progress, is one of the many medical innovations currently being used to help psychologists determine causes for various changes in behavior.

Will these developments remove the need for psychological testing? Not in the foreseeable future. A better understanding of how our bodies' systems influence our behavior may lead to new ways of diagnosing mental illness; however, we still need tools to measure what that behavior is. Moreover, in more common settings, such as schools and corporations, psychological testing remains the most efficient and economical method available for the general screening of large numbers of people. Ultimately, our curiosity about who we are and our need to be able to quantify intelligence, skills, and interests will continue to motivate the development and refinement of psychological tests.

APPENDIX

FOR MORE INFORMATION

MENTAL HEALTH ORGANIZATIONS

The following is a list of mental health organizations that can help you find more information about psychological testing or mental health professionals in your community who can administer psychological tests. Call or write these agencies for information about psychiatrists or counselors in your area. You can also contact your school counselor or your county mental health department for information.

American Academy of Child and Adolescent Psychiatry (AACAP)
3615 Wisconsin Avenue NW
Washington, DC 20016-3007
(202) 966-7300
http://www.aacap.org

American Counseling Association
801 North Fairfax Street, Suite 304
Alexandria, VA 22314
(800) 326-2642
http://www.counseling.org

American Psychiatric Association
Public Affairs Office, Suite 501
1400 K Street NW
Washington, DC 20005
(202) 682-6220
http://www.psych.org

American Psychological Association (APA)
750 First Street NE
Washington, DC 20002
(202) 336-5800
http://helping.apa.org

National Mental Health Association (NMHA)
1021 Prince Street
Alexandria, VA 22314-2971
(703) 684-7722
(800) 969-NMHA (6642)
http://www.nmha.org
Call or write for a list of affiliate mental health organizations in your area that can provide resources and information about treatment professionals and community clinics. (Include $1.00 for postage and handling.)

TEST PUBLISHERS

Administrators usually purchase commercially available psychological tests through the test publisher, who holds the copyright to tests that it distributes and maintains copies of tests, test manuals, and scoring keys. Many publishers have separate policies for individual and organizational purchases of tests. Individuals may be required to complete a test purchaser qualifications form that allows the publisher to determine whether the purchaser is qualified and competent to administer and interpret the test. Several test references exist that list psychological tests and their publishers. The following listing includes some of the most common:

Buros Institute for Mental Measurements
University of Nebraska Press
312 North 14th Street, P.O. Box 880484
Lincoln, NE 68588-0484
(800) 755-1105
Mental Measurements Yearbook, 13th edition (1998), includes both new and revised tests released since the last yearbook and the most popular tests. In addition to basic publishing information about each test, it includes information about the intended test audience and reviews of the tests and testing materials.
Tests in Print, fourth edition (1994), includes information about more than 3,000 tests and includes a directory of publishers. The book does not critique the tests.

Pro-Ed
8700 Shoal Creek Boulevard
Austin, TX 78757
(512) 451-3246 or (800) 897-3202
Test Critiques (updated annually) is designed as a companion volume to *Tests* (see below). The book includes information about each test's reliability, validity, and norm development. Each test is also critiqued. The book is intended for professionals as well as for those who are not familiar with test terminology.
Tests, fourth edition, contains information on thousands of tests used in psychology, education, and business. It describes the intended population for each test, as well as the test's purpose, major features, administration time, scoring method, cost and availability, and primary publisher. The book does not critique the tests.

INTELLIGENCE TESTS AND ACADEMIC ACHIEVEMENT TESTS

Bayley Scales of Infant Development (second edition), ages 1 month to 42 months: A test that provides infants and children with situations and tasks to capture their interest and produce an observable set of behavior responses. The primary value of the test is diagnosing developmental delay and planning strategies for correcting the problem.

Boehm Tests of Basic Concepts (third edition), ages 3 to 5: An individually administered test that uses color pictures to assess children's mastery of basic concepts fundamental to understanding verbal instructions in the classroom. These skills are essential for early school achievement.

Cognitive Abilities Test (Form 5), kindergarten to grade 12: An integrated series of tests designed to evaluate the individual differences among children in their development of verbal, quantitative, and spatial skills. These abilities are closely related to a child's success in school and are useful in enhancing the student's chances of success in learning.

Columbia Mental Maturity Scale (CMMS), preschool to grade 4: A 15- to 20-minute test that is administered individually and estimates the general reasoning ability of the child being studied. The tester shows the child cards containing three to five items and asks the child to identify the item that is different from or unrelated to the others.

Gray Oral Reading Test (GORT-3), ages 7 years to 18 years, 11 months: An individually administered test that provides an objective measure of growth in oral reading and aids in the diagnosis of oral reading difficulties. The reader is evaluated both in terms of the time taken to read each passage and the errors made in reading.

Henmon-Nelson Tests of Mental Ability, kindergarten to grade 12: A test that evaluates verbal and mathematical skills. This test is available in three overlapping grade levels and can be administered either individually or to a group.

Kaufman Adolescent and Adult Intelligence Test (KAIT), ages 11 to 85-plus: An individually administered battery of tests that measures general intelligence, including high-level adult tasks that require reasoning and planning ability. Because the test does not depend on fine motor coordination and motor speed, the evaluation of cognitive abilities is somewhat removed from elements that reflect motor skills.

Kaufman Tests of Educational Achievement (KTEA), ages 6 to 22: An individually administered test that evaluates reading, mathematics, and spelling skills. It is scheduled to expand to cover ages 4½ to 22 during the year 2000.

McCarthy Scales of Children's Abilities, ages 4½ to 8½: An individually administered test that uses toy-like materials and game-like tasks to assess intellectual and motor development.

Otis-Lennon School Ability Test, seventh edition, kindergarten to grade 12: A group-administered test that measures a student's abstract thinking and reasoning abilities and helps provide an understanding of a student's relative strengths and weaknesses in performing a variety of reasoning tasks.

Peabody Individual Achievement Test-Revised (PIAT-R), ages 5 to 18: An individually administered test that measures general knowledge, reading recognition, reading comprehension, spelling, mathematics, and written expression.

Slosson Full-Range Intelligence Test (S-FRIT), ages 5 to 21: An individually administered test that screens intellectual strengths and weaknesses in 20 to 35 minutes. Specific areas evaluated include verbal ability, performance, and memory.

Woodcock Reading Mastery Test-Revised (WRMT-R), kindergarten-age to adult: An individually administered test that assesses reading performance. Form G evaluates reading readiness and achievement. Form H evaluates reading achievement, as well as reading vocabulary in the areas of general reading, science/mathematics, social studies, and humanities.

PERSONALITY TESTS

Adjustment Scales for Children and Adolescents (ASCA), ages 5 to 17: A teacher rating scale used to detect emotional disturbance.

Children's Apperception Test (CAT), seventh revised edition, ages 3 to 10: Individually administered projective test that assesses children's personality using 10 drawings of animals in social situations. This test focuses on general needs and perceptions, as well as on the child's relationship with his or her family and significant others.

Connors' Rating Scales (CRS), ages 3 to 17: Brief questionnaires for parents and teachers that focus on attention, impulsivity, and social problems associated with Attention Deficit Disorder (ADD). This test is used in evaluating ADD and Attention Deficit Hyperactivity Disorder (ADHD).

Devereux Behavior Rating Scale and Devereux Scales of Mental Disorders, ages 5 to 18: Scales that assessment professionals use to evaluate the existence of behavioral or emotional problems. The scales help evaluators determine student behaviors that fall within the normal range and those that indicate a severe emotional disturbance.

Index of Personality Characteristics (IPC), ages 8 to 17: A 75-item test that provides information about the personal and social adjustment of children.

Kinetic Family Drawing, ages 6 to 17: A test in which the evaluator asks a student to draw a picture of a family doing something together. The evaluator often asks standardized or individualized questions about the drawings. This test is helpful in assessing children's perceptions of themselves, their families, and the dynamics of their family interactions.

Million Adolescent Personality Inventory, ages 13 to 18: A brief, self-report inventory designed to assess adolescent personality characteristics such as coping styles, expressed concerns, and behavioral patterns. This inventory is useful in initial evaluations of both typical and troubled adolescents.

Sentence Completion Test, ages 12 and up: A projective test that can be administered either individually or to a group, which includes 65 phrases, each one forming the first part of a sentence that the subjects must complete. Interpretation focuses on behavior reactions, needs, and environmental demands.

Social Skills Rating System (SSRS), preschool to grade 12: Behavior rating forms that are completed by the teacher, the parent, and the student. The results assess social skills, problem behaviors, and academic competence.

Student Self-Concept Scale (SSCS), grades 3 to 12: An individually or group-administered test that assesses how students feel about their abilities to perform in academic and social settings and measures their general self-concept.

APPENDIX

BIBLIOGRAPHY

Armstrong, Thomas. *In Their Own Way: Discovering and Encouraging Your Child's Personal Learning Style.* New York: G. P. Putnam's Sons, 1987.

Blake, Toni, ed. *Enduring Issues in Psychology.* San Diego: Greenhaven Press, 1995.

Carson, Robert C., James N. Butcher, and James C. Coleman. *Abnormal Psychology and Modern Life*, 8th ed. Glenview, Ill.: Scott Foresman, 1988.

DeAngelis, Tori. "ADA Confounds Use of Psychological Testing." *APA Monitor* (November 1995). Available at http://www.apa.org/monitor/nov95/medexams.

Gould, Stephen Jay. *The Mismeasure of Man.* New York: Norton, 1981.

Hales, Robert E., et al., eds. *APP Textbook of Psychiatry*, 2nd ed. Washington, D.C.: American Psychiatric Press, 1994.

"Intelligence: Knowns and Unknowns." Report of a task force established by the Board of Scientific Affairs of the American Psychological Association, Washington, D.C., August 7, 1995.

"Learning Disabilities." NIH Publication No. 93-3611, National Institutes of Health, Bethesda, Md., September 1993.

Murphy, Kevin R., and Charles O. Davidshofer. *Psychological Testing: Principles and Applications.* Upper Saddle River, N.J.: Prentice-Hall, 1991.

Pehl, Jeanmarie, and Judy K. Werder Sargent. *Test Your Child: Birth to Six.* Philadelphia: Camino Books, 1995.

Pierangelo, Roger, and Robert Jacoby. *Parents' Complete Special Education Guide: Tips, Techniques and Materials for Helping Your Child Succeed in School and Life.* West Nyack, N.Y.: Center for Applied Research in Education, 1996.

"Psychological Testing," "Personality Assessment," and "Personality." *Encyclopedia Britannica Online.* Available at http://members.eb.com/.

Shore, Milton F., P. J. Brice, and B. G. Love. *When Your Child Needs Testing.* New York: Crossroad Publishing, 1992.

Smith, Samuel. *The Ideas of the Great Psychologists.* New York: Barnes and Noble, 1983.

Wade, Carole, and Carol Travis. *Psychology,* 3rd ed. New York: HarperCollins College, 1993.

APPENDIX

FURTHER READING

Baron, Renee. *What Type Am I? Discover Who You Really Are.* New York: Penguin, 1998.

Berens, Linda V., and Dario Nardi. *The 16 Personality Types: Descriptions for Self-Discovery.* Santa Clara, Calif.: Telos Press, 1999.

Bolles, Richard Nelson. *What Color Is Your Parachute? 2000.* Berkeley, Calif.: Ten Speed Press, 1999.

Butcher, James Neal. *A Beginner's Guide to the MMPI-2.* Washington, D.C.: American Psychological Association, 1999.

Eysenck, H. J., and Darrin Evans. *Know Your Child's IQ.* New York: Penguin, 1998.

Jacobsen, Mary-Elaine. *Liberating Everyday Genius.* New York: Ballentine, 1999.

Montagu, Ashley, ed. *Race and IQ.* New York: Oxford University Press, 1999.

Murphy, Elizabeth. *The Developing Child: Using Jungian Types to Understand Children.* Palo Alto, Calif.: Consulting Psychologists Press, 1992.

Piirto, Jane. *Understanding Those Who Create.* Scottsdale, Ariz.: Gifted Psychology Press, 1998.

Sher, Barbara, and Barbara Smith. *I Could Do Anything If I Only Knew What It Was: How to Discover What You Really Want and How to Get It.* New York: Bantam Doubleday Dell, 1995.

Tieger, Paul D., and Barbara Barron-Tieger. *Nature by Nurture: Understand Your Child's Personality Type—And Become a Better Parent.* Boston: Little, Brown, 1997.

Zeidner, Moshe, and Robert Most, eds. *Psychological Testing: An Inside View.* Palo Alto, Calif.: Consulting Psychologists Press, 1992.

APPENDIX

GLOSSARY

Administration: the way a test is presented or given to its subjects.

Bias: a preference or inclination, especially one that prevents impartial judgment.

Extrovert: a person who seeks out the company of others and enjoys social contacts. Carl Jung first introduced this term in 1921.

Inferiority complex: a pattern in which an individual's personality revolves around trying to make up for some perceived deficiency or lack.

Intelligence: a person's ability to adapt to his or her environment. The abilities to solve problems, adjust to new situations, and learn new skills contribute to a person's intelligence.

Introvert: a person who withdraws into him- or herself and avoids social interaction. Carl Jung first introduced this term in 1921.

IQ: Intelligence Quotient—the sum of a subject's mental age divided by his or her chronological age and multiplied by 100. The IQ is one way of measuring intelligence.

Natural observation: studying behavior by observing and recording events as they naturally occur in life.

Norms: a representation of what the standard, normal, or expected performance on a test should be. Norms are created and refined while a test is being developed.

Objective tests: tests that ask a series of specific questions designed to be answered from a limited selection of provided choices. Subjects typically choose between "yes" and "no" responses or select two or more short phrases. Administrators can give these tests in a group setting and can score them relatively quickly.

Personality: how a person views his or her own thoughts, feelings, and behaviors and those of others and how those thoughts, feelings, and behaviors help a person adapt to various environments and circumstances. Each individual has a unique personality.

Projective tests: tests that are based on a set of standardized stimuli such as inkblots or ambiguous images. These tests are usually administered one-on-one and give the subject greater freedom in responding than do objective tests.

Psychological assessment: a psychological evaluation based on the results of two or more tests administered to the same subject. Each test assesses a specific type of information. Other tools that professionals use in a psychological assessment include interviews with the individual and his or her family and friends; direct observation; and examination of school, medical, and other records.

Psychological testing: the systematic use of tests to quantify human behavior, abilities, and problems and to make predictions about future performance.

Reliability: how well a test produces the same results under the same set of circumstances in the same person. Reliable tests produce reasonably consistent results.

Self-reporting technique: testing method in which subjects provide information about themselves. Self-reporting may skew results, since subjects may report what they want other people to perceive or they may have a distorted view of their own character and abilities.

Standardized tests: tests with carefully defined procedures for administration and scoring that allow them to be administered in a uniform or "standard" way. Their content is selected through a rigorous process.

Traits: attitudes and qualities that an individual tends to show in most situations. People can generally be expected to act, think, or feel a certain way if they possess certain common, measurable traits.

Unconscious: the part of a person's mental ability that lies beyond conscious control or awareness. Freud first introduced this term at the end of the 19th century.

Validity: the degree to which a test actually measures whatever it was designed to measure.

APPENDIX

INDEX

ACT. *See* American College Test
ADA. *See* Americans with Disabilities Act
Adler, Alfred, 52, 53
AGCT. *See* Army General Classification Test
Allport, Gordon, 45, 50
American College Test (ACT), 38–39
Americans with Disabilities Act (ADA), 74, 77
aptitude tests, 25
Army General Classification Test (AGCT), 37

Binet, Alfred, 24, 33, 37, 42, 59

CAI. *See* Career Assessment Inventory
California Achievement Test (CAT), 15
California Personality Inventory, 75
Campbell Interest and Skill Survey (CISS), 72
Career Assessment Inventory (CAI), 71, 72
CAT. *See* California Achievement Test
Cattell, Raymond B., 45, 50–52
children
    determining whether to test, 61–63
    purpose of testing, 59–61

testing of, 9, 65–69
value of testing, 63–65
CISS. *See* Campbell Interest and Skill Survey
Comprehensive Test of Basic Skills, 15
computed tomographic scanning (CT scan), 81, 82
confidentiality, 10, 23, 39–41, 67, 68
Confucius, 19
CT scan. *See* computed tomographic scanning

Darwin, Charles, 42
direct observation, 65

EEGs. *See* electroencephalograms
electroencephalograms (EEGs), 81–82
employment, interest and skills testing for, 9, 14, 26, 72–74
extroverts, 53
Eysenck, Hans Jürgen, 45, 52

Freud, Sigmund, 47–49, 52–53

Galen, 32, 46–47
Galton, Sir Francis, 32–33
Gould, Stephen Jay, 42

Holtzman Inkblot Test, 54

inferiority complex, 53
intelligence, 14, 26, 46
    defined, 29, 31
    theories of, 32–33
intelligence quotient (IQ), 23–24,
    33–35
intelligence testing, 33–35
    of adults, 36–37
    bell curve in, 35–36, 59
    biases in, 31, 36, 38, 40–42, 52
    and chronological aging, 36
    and comparison, 31–32
    criticism of, 39–43
    group, 37–39
interest testing, 9, 25, 26
    and career choices, 71–72
    criticism of, 74–77
    and life changes, 72
introverts, 53
Iowa Test of Basic Skills, 15
IQ. *See* intelligence quotient
IQ tests. *See* intelligence testing

Jackson Vocational Interest Survey
    (JVIS), 71
Jung, Carl, 52–53
JVIS. *See* Jackson Vocational Inter-
    est Survey

KOIS. *See* Kruder Occupational
    Interest Survey
Kruder Occupational Interest Sur-
    vey (KOIS), 71

magnetic resonance imaging
    (MRI), 82
MAT. *See* Metropolitan Achieve-
    ment Test
Metropolitan Achievement Test
    (MAT), 15
Minnesota Multiphasic Personality
    Inventory (MMPI), 25, 55–57,
    59, 77

Mismeasure of Man, The (Gould),
    42
MMPI. *See* Minnesota Multiphasic
    Personality Inventory, 55
MMPI-2, 57
MRI. *See* magnetic resonance
    imaging
Myers-Brigg Type Indicator, 77

natural observation, 19–21
norms, 17, 32

objective tests, 25, 54, 74
Ogbu, John, 40–41

personality, 9, 14
    defined, 45–46
    theories of, 46–53
    and traits, 49–52
personality tests, 25
    criticism of, 51–52, 55
    objective, 55–57
    projective, 54–55
    purpose of, 53–54, 57
    reliability and validity of, 57
    self-reporting technique in,
        56
PET. *See* positron emission tomog-
    raphy
positron emission tomography
    (PET), 81, 82
projective tests, 25–26, 54, 74
psychological assessment, 65–67
psychological testing
    administration of, 15, 17
    biases in, 9, 21, 36, 74
    characteristics of good, 14–17
    criticisms of, 9–11, 13, 21, 23
    future of, 11, 83
    history of, 19–21
    and popular culture, 23–24
    and public safety, 77
    purpose of, 9, 13–14, 79, 80

reliability and validity of, 14, 21, 24, 81
types of, 24–27

Rorschach, Hermann, 23, 54
Rorschach Inkblot Test, 23, 25, 54, 59

SAT. *See* Scholastic Assessment Tests
Scholastic Assessment Tests (SAT), 16, 17, 38–39
SCII. *See* Strong-Campbell Interest Inventory
Sheldon, W. H., 49
Simon, Theodore, 24, 33
standardized tests, 15–17
Stanford Achievement Test, 15
Stanford-Binet test, 33, 35, 36, 59
Stern, William, 33
Strong, Edward K., 71
Strong-Campbell Interest Inventory (SCII), 71
Strong Vocational Interest Blank (SVIB), 71

SVIB. See Strong Vocational Interest Blank
SVIB-SCII, 71

TAT. *See* Thematic Apperception Test
Terman, Lewis, 33, 42
Thematic Apperception Test (TAT), 54–55, 59

unconscious, the, 47

WAIS. *See* Wechsler Adult Intelligence Scale
Wechsler, Dr. David, 36, 37
Wechsler Adult Intelligence Scale (WAIS), 36, 59
Wechsler Intelligence Scale for Children (WISC), 37
Wechsler Preschool and Primary Scale of Intelligence (WPPI), 37
WISC. *See* Wechsler Intelligence Scale for Children
WPPI. *See* Wechsler Preschool and Primary Scale of Intelligence

APPENDIX

PICTURE CREDITS

page
8: Vannucci Foto-Services/FPG
10: © Joseph Nettis/Photo Researchers
12: © Robert Finken/Photo Researchers
15: © Vanessa Vick/Photo Researchers
16: Popperfoto/Archive Photos
18: The Andy Warhol Foundation, Inc./Art Resource, NY
20: © Shirley Zeiberg/Photo Researchers
22: © Telegraph Colour Library/FPG
26: © Will and Deni McIntyre/Photo Researchers
28: © VCG 1999/FPG
30: Lambert/Archive Photos
34: © Mary Evans Picture Library/Photo Researchers
38: © Joseph Szabo/Photo Researchers
40: © Jeff Isaac Greenberg/Photo Researchers
44: Art Resource

48: Archive Photos
51: Free Library of Philadelphia
55: AP/Wide World Photos
56: © Shirley Zeiberg/Photo Researchers
58: Archive Photos
60: © Richard Hutchings/Photo Researchers
61: Archive Photos
62: © Kenneth Murray/Photo Researchers
66: © Robert A. Isaacs/Photo Researchers
70: © Barbara Rios/Photo Researchers
73: © VCG 1998/FPG
75: AP/Wide World Photos
76: Photo Researchers
78: AP/Wide World Photos
80: © Richard T. Nowitz/Photo Researchers
82: Free Library of Philadelphia
83: AP/Wide World Photos

Senior Consulting Editor Carol C. Nadelson, M.D., is president and chief executive officer of the American Psychiatric Press, Inc., staff physician at Cambridge Hospital, and Clinical Professor of Psychiatry at Harvard Medical School. In addition to her work with the American Psychiatric Association, which she served as vice president in 1981–83 and president in 1985–86, Dr. Nadelson has been actively involved in other major psychiatric organizations, including the Group for the Advancement of Psychiatry, the American College of Psychiatrists, the Association for Academic Psychiatry, the American Association of Directors of Psychiatric Residency Training Programs, the American Psychosomatic Society, and the American College of Mental Health Administrators. In addition, she has been a consultant to the Psychiatric Education Branch of the National Institute of Mental Health and has served on the editorial boards of several journals. Doctor Nadelson has received many awards, including the Gold Medal Award for significant and ongoing contributions in the field of psychiatry, the Elizabeth Blackwell Award for contributions to the causes of women in medicine, and the Distinguished Service Award from the American College of Psychiatrists for outstanding achievements and leadership in the field of psychiatry.

Consulting Editor Claire E. Reinburg, M.A., is editorial director of the American Psychiatric Press, Inc., which publishes about 60 new books and six journals a year. She is a graduate of Georgetown University in Washington, D.C., where she earned bachelor of arts and master of arts degrees in English. She is a member of the Council of Biology Editors, the Women's National Book Association, the Society for Scholarly Publishing, and Washington Book Publishers.

Dwayne E. Pickels is an award-winning reporter with the *Greensburg (Pa.) Tribune-Review*. A magna cum laude graduate of the University of Pittsburgh, where he cofounded the literary magazine *Pendulum*, Dwayne won a Pennsylvania Newspaper Publishers' Association (PNPA) Keystone Press Award in 1992. He currently resides in Scottdale, Pennsylvania, with his wife, Mary, and their daughter, Kaidia Leigh. The author of eight books, he is currently working on a novel based on Celtic myth and legend. In addition to writing, Dwayne enjoys outdoor excursions, including bird watching, hiking, photography, and target shooting—along with typically futile attempts at fishing.